GLASGOW
FOREVER

GLASGOW FOREVER

JIM KEENAN

ALBYN PRESS

SCOTTISH
FICTION

Made and printed
in Great Britain
and published by
ALBYN PRESS
Whittingehame House
Haddington, East Lothian

ISBN 0284/98815/4

*My thanks to Lord Provost Robert Gray,
the City of Glasgow District Council,
and Elspeth King of the People's Palace*

DEDICATED TO
Jessie, and her Dad, Murdie

Contents

City Scenes

Cities force growth and make men
talkative and entertaining, but they make
them artificial. — *Emerson*

THE TWIN TENEMENT Cathedral Court boasted two self-contained washhouses, a quite progressive feature in this rather dull, depressing and rapidly decaying district near central Glasgow. Each had an adjoining highly polished tarmacadam clothes-drying patch. Both structures were mounted on top of two of the highest tenement properties in Townhead. The Court was located quite near to the Glasgow Cathedral; hence its somewhat elevated title!

Catering for approximately seventy working-class families, it would seem perfectly natural to assume that the toil-worn housewife and young mothers would have taken full advantage of these unique laundering facilities. The alternative communal Glasgow corporation washhouse known locally as the "Steamie" provided an array of ultra modern equipment. But it had to be paid for, and money was a notoriously scarce commodity in the early nineteen-thirties. But there were glaringly obvious drawbacks to using the tenement washing services.

For a start, the drying patch included serried ranks of stinking chimney pots, all of them belching smoke and soot from the coal fires and gleaming cooking ranges in the room and kitchen houses below. The scrupulously polished kitchen fire hearth was the pride and joy of the Townhead housewife and comparisons were constantly being made between envious dwellers.

The grimy soot-crusted chimney stacks were mounted on raised brick-built pedestals in groups of seven, and access for the chimney sweep was by a short, rusty, well-hooked ladder. In fairness to the generally smoke ridden murky atmosphere, the view from the roof of the Court, in Rottenrow, was quite impressive, especially to the local kids whose vision of the world

9

rarely exceeded a tramcar ride to Bishopbriggs or the fresh green fields of Milngavie.

The most prominent local landmark was the Glasgow Royal Infirmary which, from this vantage point, seemed to be located smack in the centre of the Necropolis. In fact, the Royal and the cemetery were no more than a thousand yards distant and to the north. Looking south from the flat roof top beyond Duke Street Prison and the Tolbooth Steeple at Glasgow Cross lay the rolling panorama of Cathkin Braes — that was the countryside as far as the Townhead kids were concerned.

The Lum

A ploughman on his legs is higher than a
gentleman on his knees   — *Franklin*

JOE was a hard grafter. He had to be, in a district which, in the thirties, had the dubious reputation of the highest unemployment rate in the city. Joe had a wife, a cat and six children to feed. When employed legitimately Joe was a time served slater and plasterer with the lucrative additional qualification of chimney-sweep.

In the long summer evenings of 1934, Joe would leap off the slowly moving Springburn tramcar at the corner of High Street and Rottenrow, just opposite the prison wall, after finishing his daily graft at five o'clock. Although burdened with his canvas tool bag containing float, trowels and hammers, he had performed this trapeze act for donkeys' years, since the tramcar had just struggled up the Bell o' the Brae, trailing bright sparks on the lines from George Street. His descent from the platform was hardly spectacular; anyway, the driver could continue his journey to the next stop at Macleod Street without having to apply his brakes.

Joe strolled up Rottenrow, resembling one of the "Clay Men" characters currently showing in the Flash Gordon serial at the nearby Carlton Cinema. Wearing a bunnet as big as a doo-lander and a wine mopper's raincoat, he was covered in finely powdered cement from his big ear-flapping bunnet to his scruffy, tackety boots. His spectre-like appearance would have scared the shit out of any strange kids in the neighbourhood!

Young Andy McCormack, hurtling down the steep slope of lower Rottenrow from Collins Street, on his guidie (a plank of wood on a set of pram wheels) was about nine years old and was as fat as a slate. Flashing past, Joe indicated that he would need his assistance later on, after teatime. Joe lived on the second storey of the five high tenement, just one up on Andy's house. As the only authorised chimney sweep locally, Joe's services were always in great demand since the briquette and coal fire was virtually the only source of home heating in the Townhead — or in Glasgow for that matter.

Most of the coal had been laboriously scraped — or stolen — from the disused bing at Garngad and other exhausted pits in the area. He charged sixpence for sweeping a lum, so that his steady sideline job could be quite remunerative, although the average householder could only afford to have it done once a year and always in the summer months. The chimney sweep and the house painter were probably the only grade of tradesmen who could force an edge on the illegal home renovation market. The local means test examination board saw to that! The other skilled men — fitters, plumbers and shipwrights — had been unceremoniously dumped out of the steel mills, construction sites, and shipyards and had been on the breadline for some time quite apart from the thousands of unskilled labouring men.

The Black Shift

JOE and young Andy met as arranged on the stairhead at half past six. Of course Joe still looked like a Gorbals tramp. Some folk swore to Christ that he slept like that — floppy greasy raincoat and the other manky accoutrements. Andy helped Joe carry his graith upstairs to the rooftop. He was dressed as usual, in his parish tweeds — there was nothing else he could have worn. Issued by the Education Authority, subject to the strict application of a deprived family means test, the most that could be said for the outfit was that it was hard-wearing. It had to be. It was intended to last for a year!

A pair of mottled leather heavy duty studded ankle boots,

black woollen stockings with two distinguishing white rings at the top for decoration, a set of grey combined vest and pants — known as combies — and two-piece short trousered suit with dog tooth pattern and barbed wire texture. Political commentators referred to it as the uniform of the junior proletariat.

The flue to be cleaned led to Miss McDabbitie's flat, a single end on the ground floor, and therefore a bloody nuisance if ever there was one. As Joe often remarked, a sweep would hardly make a mistake in one of the big posh country mansions in Pollokshields or in Bearsden, but to make the wrong lum selection in a working-class tenement block could prove calamitous. Terrible vengeance would be wreaked on a careless chimney sweep by an irate Townhead housewife.

Traditionally, before commencing work, Joe and the laddie were offered a mug of sweet tea and a slice of bread, liberally spread with Co-operative rhubarb jam, the cheapest on the market. The householder then left them to get on with the job, usually visiting the next door neighbour if they happened to be on speaking terms. The first task was to lower the sliding smoke boards so that as much as possible of the yawning fireplace was closed. In Cathedral Court, the fire hearth was like a black chasm. A big moth-eaten dust sheet was then slung over the fireplace opening and tied at the top to the projecting gas mantle bracket.

It was absolutely essential to ensure that the edges of the sheet were securely trapped all round.

The sheet itself was as big, black and wide as a nun's cassock. All the available domestic items of reasonable weight were brought into play for this most important task. Certain equipment was standard in the average Townhead household.

Most working-class homes had a "piggy" — a polished stone hot-water bottle with a snout-like carrying handle — and every one had a big heavy smoothing iron.

Andy's primary function was to make damned sure that nothing escaped from the innards of that big black sheet, which when thoroughly trapped all round, billowed and blew like the mainsail of a sailing ship in a gale force wind due to the down-draught from the chimney top. To the uninitiated, that bulging sheet was live! When everything was battened down to Joe's satisfaction he would then dawdle up the five storey stairway to the rooftop.

Loosening his bundle of flexible drain rods, he would attach his big circular hard bristle lum brush — ready for insertion. "A-A-A-HOOO"! The memory of that demonic roar from the fat black belly of the soot sheet would be imprinted on Andy's mind for the rest of his natural life!

Joe's hellish bellow echoing down the whole length of the long chimney vent was confirmation that he had found the right lum. Invariably, a few elderly residents had the living daylights scared out of them while sitting peaceably toasting a slice of bread at their fire bars before Joe had made the right selection. To have worked on the wrong flue didn't bear thinking about!

Andy, with a Tarzan-like yodel from the back court, would indicate to Joe that he had made the right choice. On forcing his tightly meshed brush down the shaft the heaving black sheet bulged outwards like a pregnant pig with spurts of soot scattering about all over the kitchen like a myriad of black fireworks. When Joe appeared on the scene the transformation was magical.

He had gone upstairs resembling a flour miller and now looked like a coal miner who had come straight from the pit face! Enveloping as much of the soot as possible in the sheet, Joe, leaving Andy to take all the snash from the customer, beat a hasty retreat next door for his tanner before dumping the lot in the tenement midden.

The Steamie

What we call progress is the exchange of
one Nuisance for another Nuisance
— *Havelock Ellis*

No, THE DRYING AREA CONDITIONS on the flat rooftop were definitely not conducive to a lily white washing; especially during a chimney cleaning session. And the Townhead housewife, against all the odds of a polluted atmosphere, insisted on the production of a spotlessly clean laundry.

Although the roof top wash-house included several wall-mounted zinc sinks and a sturdy stone-lined coal-fired boiler, experience had demonstrated that the possibility of displaying an immaculate laundry was remote indeed. So it was rarely used unless economic necessity dictated. The whole edifice was eventually left to decay and ultimately served as an ideal nesting area for the profusion of pouting pigeons.

The Steamie was the housewive's choice.

The Townhead Public Baths and Wash House were included in the same building as the Collins Institute, the Social and Recreation Centre of the well-known Glasgow publishers. They were located halfway along the street named after the publishing house, and about five hundred yards from the entrance to Cathedral Court.

Quite imposing in its way and fronted by a few cylindrical stone pillars, it faces almost directly on to Provands Lordship (the oldest house in Glasgow) and the Cathedral itself. The Corporation wash house provided symmetrical rows of galvanised washing cubicles ranged alongside powerful clothes-drying compartments.

The drying section, a metallic frame which banked the soaking wet, newly-washed clothes on parallel tubular rails, was manually operated, and when loaded was pushed into a vast superheated chamber on slide rails.

In the Steamie, everything required to produce a virgin white washing was readily available. Big red strong-smelling throat-catching lumps of carbolic soap, bleach, a selection of colour dyes, piping hot water, mangles, high speed centrifugal clothes driers, and most important of all, the opportunity for a housewives' rendezvous and a communal natter.

The whole environment of the Steamie contributed in no small measure to alleviating the drudgery of day-to-day clothes cleaning for the working-class mothers.

The Steamie's ideal facilities were booked on a one hour basis on any working weekday, and till noon on a Saturday. Andy's mother rented a two hour stint every Tuesday — traditionally "half-shut" day — from ten till twelve, finishing the chore just in time to feed Andy and his two brothers at school dinner-time. Andy's regular task on a Tuesday was to transport the finished wash to his home in the Court. Usually he trundled the big zinc bath on his guidie. Others quickly took advantage of Andy's mode of conveyance and was able to acquire a few hard earned coppers, since invariably he had to hump the bath or wicker clothes basket up the tenement stairs.

14

The men of Townhead, most of whom were unemployed, had the time and the inclination to assemble in groups, usually in the pubs, local labour clubs at open air political meetings, or in unemployed demonstrations.

There were very few comparable opportunities for the harassed women of the district, whose drab lives were generally centred on the kitchen sink, cooking stove or stair washing. In fact, in order to maintain a fairly reasonable standard, Andy's mother was forced to scrub the well-worn skelf-ridden class room floors at the local school — and for a mere pittance.

So the steamie served as an ideal source of information and gossip — births, deaths, marriages, and details about the highest available returns on pledges from the rash of local pawnbrokers.

The tremendous heat in the Steamie generated by the farting spurts of high pressure steam valves, the smooth but slithery concrete floor, interwoven with fast-flowing rivulets of gurgling hot soapy water and the complete lack of ventilation in the glass-paned roof, created a temperature akin to the inside of a Turkish Bath.

All this, combined with the incessant clanging of heavy steel drying doors and the high-pitched screaming of the rotating centrifugals was a quite terrifying experience to the stranger.

The washerwomen, operating in conditions of this intense temperature level, were forced to adapt a suitable mode of dress — or undress — that afforded some degree of comfort and became instantly recognisable as the uniform of the Steamie. This involved the absolute minimum of everyday dress, and, in order to maintain a modicum of decency, consisted of a big red rubber apron looped with string around the neck, and stretching to the exposed ankles.

Miraculously, conversation could still be conducted amidst the racket of pounding machinery and swishing steam between the cubicles of washing cells, as these were separated by open mesh liners resembling the bat wing doors of a western saloon bar.

The whole totally enclosed area, viewed from above, interspersed with a complicated network of pipes, clouds of steam, and hosts of rubber-clad dervish-like washerwomen, could best be compared to a scene from Dante's Inferno.

But it was hygienic.

The housewife felt a deep sense of pride in having overcome yet another obstacle in her depressing daily drudgery.

The crisp, white, fresh laundry cracked gaily in the midday breeze as she left the Steamie.

Jingoism

> For it's Tommy this an' Tommy that,
> and
> Chuck 'im out, the brute!
> But it's Saviour of 'is country
> When the guns begin to shoot!
> — *Kipling*

ANDY'S FATHER was just one of the many thousands of statistics on the unemployment register in Glasgow. He had been a regular soldier of the Queens' Own Cameron Highlanders, having signed for nine years with the colours and three with the reserves. He had enlisted with countless others in order to escape from the blight of mass unemployment and defeatism.

Most of his active service had been spent in Rawalpindi, Karachi and the Khyber Pass, where his main occupation had been concerned with the ruthless suppression of Indian hunger demonstrations. Andy, with his formative young mind, had been regaled from an early age with the grisly tales of glory in India, of his Dad having been in the forefront of bayonet charges on the "Frontier", and where the ideal method of quelling a rising was to use the butt of the .303 on the black skull.

His dad claimed that this was quicker and cleaner in the long run. "There were thousands of the black bastards, son, and this was the most effective way to deal with them. The bayonet was O.K. but sometimes it would get jammed between the ribs." It occurred to Andy that if the rapidly developing militancy and sense of revolt continued in Glasgow, then his Dad was liable to suffer the same treatment that he had inflicted on the Indian people — and maybe at the hands of his ex-colleagues in the "Ladies from Hell"!

Andy's uncle had been an associate of the Socialist, John Maclean, and had often heard him proclaim that "there's always a worker at both ends of the bayonet." He sensed a connection here somewhere. Now he used his Dad's army kilt as a guiser's outfit at Halloween.

The Outcome

Religion is the opium of the people
— *Karl Marx*

THE LOCAL AUTHORITY had a meeting and conference hall in the basement of one of the tenement blocks in Cathedral Court. It was available for hire, and at that time its facilities seemed to be the monopoly of the Independent Labour Party. Currently, it was being used as a base for the Order of Rechabites. Occasionally, their meetings included a session of "still" picture slides demonstrating — quite forcibly — the effects of over-indulgence on family life.

The hard-pressed mothers of Townhead often encouraged their offspring to attend. Some of them did so, since the reward for quiet, rapturous attention to detail was a wee poke of stale buns.

Their advocacy of the evils of strong drink seemed to have little or no effect on the menfolk.

The men, including Andy's Father, spent most of their nights lounging about the street corners at Taylor Street, Rottenrow, or lying sprawled out on the concrete steps of the Townhead school. Cheap drink was always in plentiful supply in the pubs and clubs which proliferated in Townhead. And if the monetary wherewithal was in short supply, a resourceful man could whip a pint bottle of milk from a doorstep and inject it with a surge of coal gas from the stairhead light bracket. The Townhead Cocktail!

When the pubs disgorged their befuddled customers on a Saturday night at nine o'clock — and none too gently — all hell would be let loose at some of the more disreputable establishments. Inspired by cheap wine and "Red Biddy", and their past glorious experiences as Soldiers of the King, shouting religious or patriotic jingoistic slogans, they would lend comradely

17

support to each other while pitching drunkenly from one side of the street to the other.

Innocent passers-by were ruthlessly cast aside in the victorious march homewards!

Pitched battles and vicious bottle-wielding fights erupted. Inevitably the remnants of their spites and hatreds were vented on their wives and families when they finally crawled home. Andy, wide awake in bed with his young brother, grew to fear and detest the screaming, drunken renderings of "The Sash" ot "Kevin Barry" drifting ominously down Rottenrow. He knew, instinctively, that the outcome of the Rangers and Celtic football match could determine the fate of his mother when the family breadwinner arrived home, paralytic and smeared with sickness, blood and stale booze.

Childhood Recreation

Ah! happy years! once more
who would not be a boy!
— *Byron*

FUN AND AMUSEMENT for Andy and his pals had to be self-created. It certainly wasn't served on a silver platter in Townhead in the early thirties.

Economic and social depression couldn't deter the enjoyment to be found in the back courts and seedy alleyways of the district.

The grass simply didn't grow in Rottenrow. The nearest greenery was at Cathedral Square, between the Necropolis and the north end of Duke Street Prison. The grass grew in the prison precincts though.

From the flat roof top of the Court tenement, the prisoners could be seen working in the flower beds and vegetable plots during the warm summer evenings. And in their innocence, Andy and his mates envied them in their labours over the forbidding high wall.

The Necropolis was an ideal playground where childish, dare-devil plots could be hatched, and expeditions made into the ancient tombs and catacombs.

It was situated on a prominent grassy mound, and the approach to the pinnacle was by a series of undulating, gravelled terraces alongside some of the oldest gravestones in Glasgow.

Although it was located in one of the busiest parts of Glasgow, the city sounds never seemed able to penetrate the peace and solitude that pervaded the Necropolis, especially on the higher levels.

It was almost as though some form of invisible spiritual barrier had been erected to create immunity from the clank and screech of nearby tramcars, the roar of motor buses in John Knox Street, and the incessant clip-clop of horses' hooves drawing railway carts up the steep slope of High Street into Castle Street.

Ironically, the green pastures of the secluded Necropolis was utilised as an excellent rendezvous for the Townhead courting fraternity!

The Swamp

FURTHER AFIELD, to the north of Glebe Street and Parliamentary Road was, without doubt, the most attractive and sought-after playground in the whole area — the "Stinky Ocean". To venture there was a challenge accepted only by the most foolhardy and brave of hearts!

Covering an area of about one and a half acres, the Stinky Ocean consisted of a morass of varying deep and shallow pools of raw carbolic, sulphuric and other acids, and a host of other obnoxious chemicals, raw sewage, stagnant, stinking green water, in addition to all known forms of expired life. The latter category included dogs and cats and giant water rats — which in some cases were very much alive!

This completely unprotected swamp had been formed over the years by effluent and unwanted pollution from local chemical industries whose owners claimed that it was not possible to dispose of it in the proper manner due to the high costs involved.

The possibility of being drowned, suffocated, or poisoned was always present.

This swamp and the adjoining Monkland and Forth and

Clyde Canals had claimed numerous human lives, many of them having been young children.

The "Ocean" was gruesome. Therein lay the challenge confronting the average headstrong Townhead schoolboy. The aura of mystery demanded investigation, and there was certainly no shortage of cocksure triers.

A raft of corrugated iron sheets, and makeshift oars, usually scrounged from the sides of a barrel discarded by the local cooperage, were in plentiful supply among the heaps of rubbish that pockmarked the surrounding area for miles around.

The ploy was to successfully navigate the putrid swamp with its constantly changing but consistently dangerous geographical features.

Andy's two chinas, Gordon and Dougie, were as chalk and cheese, poles apart in both character and physical appearance.

Gordon, tall, slim and with girlish brown eyes, and jet black immaculately combed wavy hair, was completely reserved by nature. In fact, he had been coerced into being involved at all in such a crazy adventure. He detested the Parish tweeds and refused point blank to wear the ghastly uniform. He made sure that his personal gear lasted long enough to avoid being classified as a recipient of local authority charity.

Dougie! Now he was some man if ever there was one! He lived in the High Street, a few closes up from Duke Street, and spent most of his mischievous trouble-making playing time in 79 Collins Street or the Sculptors Yard in Cathedral Street. He was, without doubt, the most unorthodox and cheekiest bastard of a boy in Townhead — and that was some accolade! If he could have been classified politically, Dougie was a born Anarchist.

Arrogant, he conformed to nothing, and resolutely spurned the few basic rules of behaviour that existed among the kids from Townhead. Exceptionally tall and broad for his age group, he boasted a fierce looking Mohican hairstyle long before the fashion had been introduced into the City of Glasgow.

Inevitably, he was the first to start stirring the shit in the Stinky Ocean when the lads finally ventured forth. Once they were afloat on the flimsy raft Dougie, without any prior warning, made a grab for a floating mangy brown tail, pulled a big sodden cat from the slimy green depths, and started swinging the corpse in ever increasing circles, showering the lads with putrid muddy water and flying fur.

Despite a hail of repeated warnings and threatening oaths he continued his mad prancing around on the rocking raft. Finally, the cat separated from the tail and the carcass smashed Andy right across the kisser! Andy was catapaulted straight into the stinking swamp calling Dougie the stupidest bastard under the sun.

The raft overturned, dumping the whole crew into the thick, gooey mess.

Their clothing, of course was completely destroyed, and all the science of the Steamie would never have restored it. Gordon's older brothers pounced on Dougie shortly afterwards, and inflicted the most vicious tanking imaginable for having ruined Gordon's only suit.

The Rat

The man recovered of the bite,
The dog it was that died.
— *Goldsmith*

As USUAL THE team of boys were booting a tanner ball around the fairly wide expanse of Collins Street after school at four o'clock. The surface was flat, suitable for all manner of ball games, and the ten feet high double green doors in Rottenrow served as an ideal goal area. Dougie skied it over the high dyke surrounding the Corporation Hydraulic Pumping Station adjacent to the Cathedral Court tenements.

Totally enclosed by the high brown sandstone wall, the station had a vast galvanised steel reservoir, a network of water pipes, and the whole cobble-stoned complex was hoaching with big, dirty, slimy, brown water rats — some of them as big as wee dogs. The lads knew, from bitter experience, not to try to force an unauthorised entry into the yard; Big Jock, the station attendant, was not a man with whom to tamper. And Dougie knew this better than the rest. He had recently fallen foul of Jock's wrath and had received a severe kick in the arse as a reminder.

"Andy," shouted Dougie, "you're Big Jock's pal, ask him to get the ball back."

Andy, ever aware of Dougie's wily ways, was adamant. "You booted it over, away and take your own bloody rap."

Caught out, Dougie suddenly remembered that he had to go to the Welfare Centre in Glenbarr Street for his wee sister's supply of cod liver oil and malt extract; apparently she was showing the first sign of bandy legs and had to be "built up".

"Yellow bastard," roared Andy. But the ruse worked — and Andy was chosen.

Big Jock lived in the first tiled close in High Street, in a house tied to the job as Attendant. Apprehensively, Andy knocked on Jock's half-glazed door.

"Mr McKinnon, the boys have asked me to find the ball in your yard. If it's O.K. with you I could jump the dyke and get it."

"Damned sure you won't!" Jock exclaimed.

Fortunately, he had finished his tea, was in a reasonable mood, and, anyway, he preferred the official approach; something to do with the status of the job, no doubt.

"Well, I have to check the water tank level, so wait there a minute till I get the bunnet." Adjusting his checked doo-lander to his baldy nut, he and Andy meandered up to the yard entrance in Rottenrow.

It was now fairly dark and the gas-lit street lanterns' glow didn't penetrate the gloomy precincts of the yard. Jock had a solid rubber torch about a foot long. Andy's mates, by this time, were thronged on the first storey landing of the Court which was separated by spiked railings, but overlooked the pumping station.

Big Jock knew he had an audience and in accordance with his "position" dictated the route to be taken in the search for the lost ball.

Some of the lads had wee threepenny "Number Eight" hand torches and were competing with each other in the hunt. The stabbing, piercing, light beams and the cacophony of shouted instructions from the assembled unruly group of boys began to irritate Big Jock — and the rats! Previous encounters had taught the lads to recognise Jock's tendency to become annoyed and fretful; invariably he became red-faced and the bunnet was shoved to the back of the baldy crust!

Jock's torchlight finally found the ball up a length of six-inch water pipe sealed at one end with a flange. He reached in for the ball — and a rat nearly tore the end of his pinkie! "Dirty Bastard," he exploded. Jock's howl of pain created a right commotion among the lads who were by this time jumping and screaming with uncontrolled hysterical excitement.

Big Jock wasn't too pleased with this unexpected turn of events — he sensed trouble! He jammed a big steel rod up the pipe, but didn't notice that it was sealed at the end. The big brown rat cornered, and somewhat upset by the noise and flashing lights, bared its teeth and made a flying leap, all two feet of it, out of the greasy pipe.

Having already sampled Big Jock's blood, it flew straight for Andy's right shin bone just below his short Parish trouser bottoms. Gouging its razor sharp fangs into Andy's skinny shin bone, it hung there, its flailing tail lashing the cobble stones with fear and anger. Feeling the whole length of its long slimy body against his bare leg sent Andy into a blind panic and he screamed like a stuck pig!

Jock lashed out with the steel rod. The rat's teeth seemed to have interlocked around Andy's bone and didn't look as though they could detach themselves. The rod smashed the rat across the snout and its narrow skull disintegrated over Andy's leg. This was the last straw — Andy conked out!

Shouted advice from all sides didn't improve matters.

"For Christ's sake, get Andy's Maw — and an ambulance from the Royal." "Flatten the bastard, Jock!"

Repeated blows forced the rat, which still looked alive, down Andy's leg, tearing the skin and bone all the way down to his blood-filled boot. Jock finally impaled it through its belly when it had slithered to ground level.

The scene was like a butcher's shop! Andy, and his mother — she had collapsed — landed in the casualty ward of the Royal. The shin bone and skin knitted naturally, but the rat's gouge mark remained for all time.

An Early Grindstone

> I never did anything worth doing by
> accident, nor did any of my inventions
> come by accident; they came by work.
> — *Edison*

DURING THESE LEAN times the burning ambition of the kids in Rottenrow was to obtain a part-time job, either as a newsboy or on milk deliveries round the sprawl of Townhead tenements. Andy struck lucky and started as a newspaper delivery boy with one of the most popular newsagents, in Castle Street, right across from the Royal Infirmary. The proprietors were two middle-aged spinster ladies, and it was cynically assumed that Andy had exercised a wee bit charm and charisma to have won such an enviable job; with early morning and late evening deliveries, the going rate was five shillings for a seven day week. This was real progress and with tips would ease the situation at home where every penny was appreciated.

Not to be outdone, Gordon won a similar type of job in George McNeil's in Cathedral Street. Dougie's reaction to this inventiveness was typical. It was degrading. It was pure bloody exploitation of child labour. He thought it was time enough to start work at fourteen after leaving school. And, on hindsight, he was probably right!

Gordon, however, was more profound. He solemnly declared that Dougie probably had a heart problem — heart bloody lazy! Actually, Dougie was genuinely concerned. He thought he recognised the first cracks in the mould of schoolboy friendships and found it a bitter pill to swallow. Nevertheless, he had a go, and it didn't involve any slogging up and down the tenement stairs.

His job only lasted an hour in the early morning at Big Nan's Co-operative Dairy in the High Street, virtually on his doorstep. The heavy wooden milk crates were delivered to the pavement at three o'clock in the morning. Dougie's job was to haul them across the three foot wide pavement, up a six inch doorstep, and into the back shop. He certainly wasn't lacking in physical strength, being as broad as a young horse. But a small degree of skill, in the wee six-inch lift, was required.

24

The crates were built four high and were recessed into each other. Each crate contained eighteen one pint bottles of milk. They were drawn by a hook cleek inserted into the opening of the bottom crate. The total weight was no problem to Dougie, who was able to draw the pile of crates across the pavement as though handling a bag of bird feathers.

On reaching the step, however, the crates were callously hauled up, couped over to an angle of about sixty degrees — and the whole bloody lot shot headlong into the street! Seventy-two pints of valuable milk were consigned to the High Street gutters and numerous marauding moggies.

The pavement was strewn with smashed glass, the cleek was thrown violently across the High Street. Big Nan heaped vicious abuse on his broad shoulders — and that was that!

For those under fourteen years of age the Education Authority had to issue a permit to work on a part-time basis and this, of course, was determined by the application of a means test of family income. Andy and Gordon qualified.

Gordon's territory centred on the vast Royal Infirmary complex. This could prove very lucrative since it included the large permanent staff of nurses and doctors, quite apart from the long standing orders placed by the patients. Tipping rates were extremely generous, especially at Christmas and New Year.

Andy's paper run was a pure slog. When he first took up the job, and for a long time afterwards, he was convinced that he was the only person awake in the deathly quiet streets of Townhead, especially during winter. He uplifted his heavy bag of newspapers at five-thirty in the morning. His first delivery was to the resident keeper of the Necropolis, straight across the quiet expanse of Cathedral Square. It was mid-December.

The roads and pavements were ice bound and treacherous, and the air would have frozen the balls off the proverbial brass monkey. Townhead was shrouded in a soot-laden fog, and the street lamps were merely ghostly blurs in the swirling misty atmosphere. Visibility was about six feet.

The Keeper's Lodge was situated inside the grounds of the Necropolis, beyond the big black wrought iron gates which fronted on to Cathedral Square. Access, of course, was over the top of the frozen ironwork. The weather was damnable, and it proved no small task to overcome the icy, protruding, ornamental metalwork, taking its toll of hand skin and exposed knees. Once over, Andy would make a sliding, skidding hundred yard dash to the keeper's letter box — and the first delivery was completed.

The next destination was the Drygate Working Mens Hotel — a model lodging house. This was best approached by perilously crossing a number of flat, ice bound gravestones which were laid so close together that the whole resembled a miniature ice-rink. Then Andy had to scale the six foot high spiked railing on to the slope of John Knox Street.

This part of the obstacle course was fraught with imminent danger and required careful thought. It wasn't the first time that a bleary-eyed pedestrian, ambling down John Knox Street to his work at five-thirty on a fog shrouded December morning, had been suddenly confronted by an apparition leaping from one of the oldest graveyards in the City of Glasgow! Had the panic stricken guy taken time to investigate he would have found that the leaping, ghostly form was Andy and the bulky newspaper bag, beating a hasty retreat from the grisly confines of the Necropolis!

By this time of course the bewildered worker had shot down the Ladywell like a bat out of Hell!

The Model – and The Jail

Blessed is he that considereth the poor.
— *Psalms, XLI, 1*

THE MODEL WAS an experience and a source of education in the realms of social and economic stagnation. The building itself was in a hell of a state of disrepair, looked dilapidated, and seemed ready to collapse around its weary inhabitants at any time. Frequented mainly by men who had been unceremoniously dumped on the industrial scrap heap, the Model was a kaleidoscope of the abject degradation that can affect a man once society has decided that his services are no longer required.

The pungent smell of frying fat and sweaty feet pervaded the whole derelict property. The centre of activity was the combined kitchen and dining area. A broad flat hot plate extended the full length of the common room, and this was fired from a heap of charcoal into a number of flaming openings in its cavernous black belly. Fuelled continuously, it operated as the cooking range as well as being the main source of heat on the lower floor. The wire-meshed upstairs dormitories and cells were heated by spluttering wax candle stumps and smoke encrusted — and illegal — paraffin lamps.

The fumes from the frying fat and grease coupled with the stench of unwashed bodies created an environment of doom and despair. Six o'clock on a mid-winter morning was the most poignant time to visit the Drygate Model — and young Andy had no option.

The Model manager read the *Glasgow Herald*. One or two of the residents read the *Daily Worker*. Was there a distinction of class even in a place like this, Andy thought? Civilised humanity in the City was at its lowest ebb in this abysmal environment.

First impressions were of doddering, sleepy-eyed unshaven men, old for their years, shuffling around in almost soleless shoes, stinking grease-stained waistcoats, and full length army greatcoats which flopped around bare ankles.

Demonstrated here, in its stark reality, was the "Penny Hang" (actually it was threepence). If a vagrant couldn't afford the full admission price, or if the cubicles were fully occupied, then he could opt for the "Penny Hang"! This consisted of a stout rope being slung between the two walls and parallel to the ever warm stove. Located about three feet from the total length of the hot plate the inmate, usually sozzled to the eyeballs, would merely slump across the hanging rope like a half-shut knife with finger tips just touching the floor and balanced precariously on his toes. If nothing else, a good sound sleep was guaranteed in a warm — albeit fusty — atmosphere.

At six o'clock, when Andy came in, the Model manager simply severed the rope and the men, tin mugs and beer bottles crashed all over the greasy floor like a set of nine-pins to the accompaniment of grumbles and loud curses!

Next on the list was at the top of Drygate, the gaunt, Victorian, Duke Street Prison. Using his bag of papers to gain height, Andy pressed the highly polished brass bell push alongside the massive steel doors which formed the main entrance. It often occurred to him that he had never yet heard that bell ringing. Perhaps the walls were too thick.

Admitted, eventually, by the Duty Screw, into the heavily cobbled courtyard, Andy, wearing the studded Parish boots, usually skidded and landed on his arse, papers flying all over the bloody place.

As time went by Andy started to think about the men, usually Socialists, who had been incarcerated within these grim walls. Men like John Maclean, Gallacher, Shinwell and others whose crimes, according to his mother, had been that they were opposed to war. How could that be classified as criminal, he wondered? At any rate, as far as he could see, their actions had been a waste of time and energy, since his newspaper headlines all spoke of war and the threat of another World War! In fact there was civil strife in Spain. Some of his Dad's mates were already talking about going there. One or two of them seemed to think that anything was bound to be an improvement on the depression and unemployment which seemed to have become a permanent way of life, and thought seriously about joining the "Terries" — or even signing on with the Regulars.

Others, though, seemed convinced that what was happening in Spain was somehow responsible for their own plight — and were prepared to do something about it!

It was all so confusing, Andy concluded.

Andy continued on his never-ending paper run. There was no time for skiving on the distribution since he had to be back home in time for his roll and plate of porridge before going to school at nine o'clock.

As he climbed the grimy tenement stairs, the spluttering stairhead gas lights reflected headline stories about National Socialists in Germany and about Fascists in Italy. Making his final delivery and starting for home, it occurred to Andy that, all things considered, it was a worthy and reasonably well paid part-time job.

He realised too that he had discovered a source of free education from the front pages of his wide selection of newspapers. Then, at nine o'clock, he and his mates lined up in the playground to receive their formal education at the local school.

Primary Education

Education makes a people easy to lead,
but difficult to drive; easy to govern, but
impossible to enslave.
— *Lord Brougham*

TOWNHEAD PUBLIC School was the main centre of activity for the children of the district and, for some of them, the school even served as a source of basic education!

The senior boys section: those aged from twelve to fourteen, was in Collins Street, just across from Collins Institute. There wasn't another like it in Glasgow. Nor was there such a varied cross-section of teachers assembled in one institute of education.

Without doubt the most controversial and dominant member of the teaching staff was Mr "Sailor" McMillan, the geography master. Sailor was a thick set, broad and swashbuckling figure of a man who, from a purely educational point of view, brooked no nonsense in his class of about twenty-five boys. However, depending on the subject being taught he occasionally displayed certain weaknesses in his character.

Of the staff, he appeared to the boys to be the most colourful, and they generally looked forward to his sessions. During his instructions he would invariably link his explanations with somewhat flighty descriptions of exaggerated exploits during his naval career. Needless to say the class, including Andy, Dougie and Gordon, raised no objection to Sailor's deviation since they usually transported their vivid youthful imaginations to the four corners of the world.

His tales were spellbinding and found avid reception in the minds of adventurous twelve or thirteen year old boys. Typically, Dougie had the measure of the Sailor. Soon after joining his class and sampling his powers of oratory Dougie's apt expression was: "A bum o' fuck if I ever heard one." He and the Sailor never did hit it off.

Sailor McMillan seemed always to take a sadistic delight in baiting wee Geordie McFarlane and exploiting the wee bloke as the classroom scapegoat. Geordie was a skinny undernourished heap of rags and bones, a right trollopy backle with the

29

inevitable Parish uniform and a permanent green snotter decorating his top lip. He was bandy legged into the bargain, which created the impression of two bent white sticks growing out of his oversized tackety boots.

The Sailor could be very vindictive indeed when he got carried away with his boasting, especially if he showed the red-nosed signs of having had a good bevvy the night before. This, coupled with the fact that he was for ever finding excuses to nip out to the staff Gents for a few drags on his Full Strength Capstan fags, made his breath stink like a navvy's oxter!

One of his favourite topics was personal hygiene. He usually related it to the need for cleanliness aboard ship in the Royal Navy, and generally introduced the subject on a stifling hot day. "Personal hygiene is just as important in the classroom as it is in the Navy," he said, casting a sidelong glance at wee Geordie — and Geordie was manky!

Dougie was quick to recognise the signs. "Dirty fat bastard, imagine him ganting about cleanliness when he stinks like a bloody skunk", he whispered, none too quietly, to Andy.

The Sailor heard the remark but he knew better than make an issue of it with Dougie.

By this time the Sailor had discarded his jacket, loosened his tie and shirt buttons, thus exposing the bulging beer belly under a sweaty semit.

"You, McFarlane!" — and wee Geordie's earhole suffered a well aimed stick of chalk. "Tell the class about the importance of cleanliness in the armpits and in the region of the groin." Bandy as he was, his wee knobbly knees were rattling like a set of drumsticks as McMillan made him shuffle, tearfully, to the front of the class.

Sailor McMillan was built like an ox, with bulging biceps on hairy arms and the tattooed topsails of a sailing ship growing out the neck of his string vest.

Alongside the Sailor, wee Geordie was hardly three feet high and was about as fat as a stalk of Blackpool rock. The wee man cowered, head bowed, in front of the embarrassed class. Dougie and Andy were raging inwardly and looked ready to explode. "Get that jacket off, McFarlane, when did you last have a good bath? What about the groin?"

"Where's ma groin, Mr McMillan? Dae ye mean ma crutch? Is it near ma wee tool?"

The Sailor blew a gasket at the roars of laughter and derision. Red faced, breathing heavily and with a distinctively effeminate squeak in his normally gruff voice, he said, "For God's sake, McFarlane, you will have to be taught some basic anatomy."

"Now lads, are you watching? Pay attention!" Grabbing wee Geordie's quivering hand he drew it towards his crutch area. "This is the groin, and it must be kept scrupulously clean by applying firm, hard strokes with a rough towel after bathing. Now George, show the class what I mean."

The boys were transfixed to their desks in anticipation, eyes boggling at poor Geordie's demonstration of the intricacies of hygiene being applied, ever more vigorously, to the Sailor's crutch.

The big beefy legs were, by now, spread wide apart and the Sailor's excited squeaky voice was becoming more pronounced. The lads couldn't quite grasp what was happening to the teacher who was now almost beetroot red in the face and whose breathing was coming in short, sharp gasps.

Wee Geordie pissed his trousers! His open top, left boot was rapidly filling up! Completely out of control, the poor wee bugger's eyes filled with tears and he burst out crying!

"Jesus Christ, Geordie's pissed his trousers!" roared Dougie, and the spontaneous howls of laughter created absolute chaos in the classroom.

The Sailor seemed to be having a fit and was hobbling, rapidly, towards the security of his high topped desk, with his legs still widespread!

The hysterical squeals from the classroom had permeated the first floor of the school. McMillan knew that he had gone just too far. Geordie, his wee mind as pure as the driven snow, slithered away, soaking wet, to the boys' cludgie for a clean up.

Infatuation

But there's nothing half so sweet in life,
as love's young dream.   — *Moore*

AMIDST THE MOTLEY of sulking humdrum teachers in Townhead Public, Miss Archibald glowed like a beacon in the

31

rather depressing environment of the school. Her presence was a constant guarantee of diversion from the subjects in question and affected all of the male staff. It also exerted a disquieting influence on the formative minds of the youthful male pupils.

The English teacher, Miss Archibald was about nineteen or twenty years old with immaculately styled and shining blonde hair which bounced in rhythm with her flouncing steps between desk and blackboard.

To the lads, this trim, slim-waisted doll of a girl resembled some of the idolised and glamorous film stars currently capturing the screen of the local Casino Cinema in Castle Street.

Andy thought her skin must be as smooth as the shiny surface of his mother's wally dogs which decorated the fireplace. The infection of her beauty strayed beyond the confines of the classroom.

There were damned few households in Townhead with a bath. The kids used the public bathtubs on the upper floor of the Steamie. When Andy and his pals were immersed in the scalding hot depths of the enamel tubs in the separated cubicles, the shouted conversations invariably centred on girls! Miss Archibald's charms, seen and imaginary, dominated the discussion in the steamy atmosphere.

It was rumoured on the school grapevine that Miss Archibald was associating with Mr Barrat, the History teacher.

Andy considered this to be a downright lie and quite preposterous. In rejecting such a ridiculous suggestion he realised, for the first time in his life, that he had fallen in love!

The Queer Man

All cruelty springs from weakness.
— *Seneca*

NOW, IF SAILOR McMillan was a boastful bum of the first order, then Barrat was the most vicious, cruel bastard of a teacher that ever trod the well worn boards of Townhead school, and it didn't help matters in that he was quite proud of his reputation.

It was well founded.

32

Andy, in his immature jealousy, refused to accept the possibility of any form of relationship, between Miss Archibald — his dream girl — and a queer bugger like "Nancy" Barrat! He was, without doubt, the most unpopular teacher on the staff. The boys hated his guts, none more so than Dougie, who had probably suffered more of Barrat's wrath than any other pupil.

Because of his sadistic — but distinctly effeminate — demeanour, Barrat had been chosen as the staff punishment teacher. His primary function in this role was to maintain a firm control over those pupils who were considered to be the most unruly and mischievous within the Secondary Division. There were a few in this category, but Dougie, true to form, was the daddy of them all!

Dougie, throughout the whole of his term in the Division, never ever completed a full, five day week at school. His expertly forged "excuse Douglas" notes from his parents had long since exhausted their effectiveness. Hence, he became a natural target for Barrat's venom. He plunked more training time than any other pupil in the Division. It was not merely coincidental that these truancies occurred during History lessons, conducted by Mr Barrat.

Occasionally, Dougie slipped up and got the programme wrong and "Nancy" Barrat fully exploited these rare situations. Once Dougie had made such an appearance he felt resigned to his fate.

"You, step up here, and be quick about it!" he called to Dougie. "Nancy" had his chair and high desk mounted on an improvised platform, thus enhancing his viewing range — and his stature, of course.

For all that when he had completed his arrogant stroll to the front of the class, hands sunk deep in his pockets, Dougie was tall enough to see the dreaded serrated leather strap coiled like a rattlesnake on the top of "Nancy's" desk.

"Get the cuffs of your jersey down to your wrists," Barrat ordered, in his high-pitched voice. Looping the cuff of his jersey over his right thumb to protect the wrist, Dougie seemed prepared to accept the punishment without any sign of an objection. However, his mates knew that this was out of the question where Dougie was concerned! It had never happened before — and wouldn't happen now!

Stretching his arm and hand outwards to their full extent,

33

without a cringe he leaned forward slightly towards "Nancy's" ear. Almost inaudibly, he whispered, "Yes, Nancy!"

Barrat blew his bloody top! He had completely lost control of his temper at such audacity in front of the assembled class.

"Get your sleeves back up to your elbows," he squealed. Silence reigned.

Dougie took five full-blooded lashings from Barrat's well directed weapon on each hand, including the wrists.

Shortly afterwards Mr Barrat was found lying between the tram lines in Duke Street. He spent an hour or so in the Royal Infirmary. It was said that while travelling homewards, after school that night, he must have been kicked by one of Wordie's cart horses as it left the High Street goods station!

Adolescent Urges

A Woman's most powerful asset is a man's imagination. — *Myself (I think)*

THE ABILITY TO participate, effectively, in after-school fisti-cuffs was considered an essential qualification in the district. A human ring, composed of gesticulating cat calling boys, was formed almost daily at four o'clock. The contest was generally organised by others and the causes were usually trivial. Once the barney had been organised, the challenger and opponent rarely backed off. To have done so, would have earned the derision of the school population.

Brave lads all! However, the courage to engage in conversation with members of the opposite sex was quite another matter! There was never any hesitation in boarding a raft on the "Stinky Ocean" or raiding the fruit stall in the market at the Candleriggs. Dougie maintained that it was a man's world. He certainly had no time for the "dames" but he was shrewd enough to recognise that Julia had her eye on Andy.

He had lost Andy's companionship for the first few hours after school, since he and Gordon had taken up the newspaper run. Dougie was, therefore, determined to sabotage this "illicit association" if possible.

34

But Julia had found a chink in Andy's hard-bitten armour. Julia's aunt, Mrs Brown, lived in the top storey flat in the tenement court. She was one of Andy's customers to whom he delivered the *Evening Times* nightly and the *News of the World* on a Sunday. Although Julia lived in McAslin Street, she often spent nights with her aunt — and every weekend.

In common with the rest of the squad, Andy had started to take an interest in the body clinging dresses, the flying skirts, and the bouncing breasts of the girls during their high flying skipping rope sessions, and their excessive leg exposure while playing in the chalked boxes with the circular paviour stone.

When lying in bed these thoughts became more pronounced. They were peculiar to himself. They were powerful. They were exciting. His visions of Julia became uncontrollable. With Julia in the forefront of his mind, he began to devour the saucy articles and provocative pictures that were prominently displayed in Mrs Brown's Sunday paper by the gas light on the top stairhead. He found himself indulging furtively in these fantasies.

The papers were paid for on a Saturday. The top storey flats ranged on a balcony, were exposed to the wind and rain. While collecting payment, if it happened to be raining, Mrs Brown would call him indoors to the kitchen while she hunted for the purse. Waiting for payment, and glancing towards the single bedroom, the dressing table mirror reflected his Julia in bed, usually naked.

Her bright shining red hair cascading on the pillow reminded Andy of a cluster of strawberries on a bank of virgin snow. He felt frightened, somehow cornered, and he wondered whether Mrs Brown was aware of his thoughts as he devoured Julia's reflection.

Julia monopolised his imagination. The main topic of conversation in the public baths and in the school toilets, was concerned with girls. This was an altogether new and fascinating dimension, and it wasn't unattractive! Was there something peculiar in this overpowering weakness? Yet he tingled with a lusty strength when he thought of Julia, and when he saw the schoolgirls deftly tucking their dresses somewhere in the mysterious region of their thighs when skipping ropes on the sultry summer evenings.

Julia was tall and slim and showing a distinctive roundness!

Her arms, face and legs bore a mass of freckles during summer time. Andy wondered if the freckles extended to the unexplored regions of her body. He was completely overcome by the possibilities. But it wasn't confined to the purely sexual opportunities.

He was in love! He wanted her to be his companion for life. He was convinced that she had been made for him! How else can true love be expressed?

When he had completed his evening newspaper run, he spent hours holed up in a derelict tenement building in Weaver Street waiting, in vain, for Julia to pass by on her way to the Court from her home in McAslin Street. Had she appeared, he knew within himself, that pure unadulterated cowardice would prevent his meeting her.

It was becoming intolerable. An approach would have to be made. The "big man" of the playground had become a weak-kneed coward, crouching in the dust-strewn loft of the deserted tenement.

He bought two bars of Cowans Milk Toffee from Miss Ward's sweet shop in Castle Street, and had them wrapped in colourful wrapping paper. He had told the lady that it was intended as a wee present for his Mother! Was he so much in love with this girl that his Mother was becoming of secondary importance? It was Friday evening. The paper run was over, thank Christ. Julia was certain to pass by — and he made his way to the attic in Weaver Street.

As he sat astride a broad ceiling beam the evening sun darted through the roof slats with sharp daggers of light. He heard the muffled sounds of laughing and screaming young children from the Swing Park across the street. He had spent many happy hours there himself — and not so long ago. He felt so far removed from childhood — and yet he had hardly entered his teenage years. Was this the "adolescence" that he had read and heard so much about? Maybe he should have been in the Swing Park, instead of cowering here contemplating a meeting with his vision of loveliness. If this was puberty, then it was bloody awkward. He didn't know whether he was coming or going.

And of course the "Thump" was there! It never stopped. The incessant, deep throated crashing thump of Boyd's steam-driven hammer in the blacksmith's shop next door had been striking a massive blow, every thirty seconds, for as long as he could remember. It had long since become fused into the local industrial environment, and was no longer noticed by the surrounding population. But Andy heard it. His mind was in a whirl. Sexual visions of Julia permeated his brain.

The cheeky, saucy chuckles from the girls in the Swing Park, interspersed with the precisely regular pulsing beat of the steam hammer. His now violent, uncontrolled images of Julia set his loins on fire and plunged his mind and body into frightening and exciting spasms of pure ecstasy.

Then he saw her! She was crossing Stirling Road — and she was on her own.

Julia was rounding the Cathedral Street corner. Finally, he plucked up enough courage to make the approach, leapt down the rickety stairway and ran towards Julia.

"Julia, I'll carry the bag, if you don't mind!"

She had a message bag of vegetables from Wallace the Fruiterer. He noticed that his voice had gained a couple of decibels as he spoke to her, and tried hard to control this sign of weakness.

He felt sure that he was making a right cock of the situation. And it didn't help matters when he noticed, for the first time, that she was slightly taller than himself. But he had never been quite so close to her before.

Julia handed over the carrier bag. The ice was broken, he thought. He reached into his hip pocket. The paper had torn and the bloody toffee bars were soft, sticky and had moulded themselves into the shape of his arse.

"I brought you a wee present," he ventured. She seemed genuinely overcome, since this was probably the first time that she had received a gift from anyone outside the family circle. And he definitely noticed a sparkle in her eyes!

The twinkle in Julia's eye clinched it. He took the plunge.

"If it's all right with your aunt, I'll take you to the Grafton tomorrow afternoon." They agreed to meet at one o'clock at St James' and Parliamentary Roads, the matinée session would commence at two.

Andy's mother had finally been able to afford to buy him his first, long trousered suit from Longstaff, the Jewish tailor in

Castle Street — through the auspices of the Provident Supply Credit Company. After all, he had worked for it, it couldn't have been arranged at a more opportune time, and he certainly wasn't going to meet Julia in the Parish monstrosity!

Surprisingly, he felt relaxed, even confident, as he waited at the corner. There was a twinge of embarrassment, though. He felt that his first "longies" were attracting a lot of attention.

"Well, what of it?" he thought. He had grown up overnight.

Julia wore a bright red coat, red platform type shoes and a simulated silk white headscarf which emphasised the glints in her burnished red hair. He thought she was walking on air! She was a picture, and Andy felt proud.

Their romance blossomed with cinema visits, outings to Springburn and Alexandra Parks, and Sunday sailings on the rowing boats at Hogganfield Loch.

Mrs Brown eventually accepted Andy as Julia's friend. This led to a "talk" between her and Andy's Mother. In fact arrangements were being made for a week's holiday to Largs by Julia and her aunt. It was agreed that if he earned enough pocket money he would accompany them! This was beyond his wildest dreams. And yet he wondered. Friendships of this nature were few and far between in the Townhead. Certainly, such relationships were never encouraged by the parents, especially at such a relatively tender age.

He never thought to inquire into the reasons for Julia spending so much time with her aunt. He knew that she had two brothers and a sister — and he hadn't yet met her parents. It may have been due to the fact that Julia's particular close in McAslin Street was pretty decrepit. Then maybe it was a problem of overcrowding — not at all uncommon in this district.

Anyway he wasn't too concerned about it, especially since his Mother and Mrs Brown were actively promoting the friendship.

It was Springtime. Andy now spent all of his spare time with 'Julia. His mates were not pleased at all. Dougie was fuming! Perhaps they were jealous. Andy was on top of the world — and he was in love! He was beginning to day-dream at school and he knew, within himself, that Julia was influencing his standard of work at School which, till then, had been of a high order. And the teachers noticed it too.

One day, just before the school holiday period commenced, and just as the arrangements for the Largs visit were going into top gear, Sailor McMillan called Andy out from his desk. He sent Andy out. His Mother had called for him, and she was waiting for him at the headmaster's office. He thought that his Dad might have got into trouble of some kind or another, or that his young brother had gone down with the scarlet fever. His Mother thought she had seen the signs on his body.

When he reached the study his Mother was obviously upset about something. But she had a permanent air of worry about her anyway, so he was not unduly concerned. She had been talking to Mr Allison and for a change he seemed to be sympathetic towards him — and his mother. Normally he was a dour bugger of a man, but this was probably due to the importance of his job.

Andy and his Mother boarded the tramcar bound for Ruchill Hospital. She wept now and then on the journey and kept dabbing her eyes with a wee, tear-soaked hankie.

He had no idea that his beloved Julia had contracted tuberculosis! He wouldn't have recognised the symptoms even if he had known. Apparently Julia had asked for him.

The first bed in the ward was surrounded by half a dozen adults, all strangers to him, except Julia's aunt who was sobbing constantly. They made way for him.

Julia was as he had seen her in her aunt's bedroom mirror, in the big white bed. But she was now much smaller.

Julia died that evening.

Changing Horses

"A horse! a horse! my kingdom for a horse!" — *Shakespeare - Richard III*

EVERYTHING WAS changing. Andy tried hard to retrace his steps. He sought the bosom of the friendly childhood companionships with Gordon, Dougie and the rest of the old gang. But the lads were drifting apart and some had actually finished school. Time had marched relentlessly forward during his diversion with Julia. The scenes of his childhood were irretrievable!

Dougie had left school, and Townhead Public heaved a sigh of relief. So did Dougie! Still flaunting the ridiculous Mohican hairstyle, he had realised his long held ambition and was now registered as a trace-horse boy at the corner of West Nile Street.

His duties involved doubling up with the railway carter on an extra heavy load. When the additional harnesses were hooked up, both horses and men would manoeuvre the heavy load up the steep incline to Buchanan Street Railway Station and to other points on the north side of the City. The wages were washers.

However, the thrill of burnishing the brass buckles with Brasso, polishing the Clydesdale's leatherwork, and topping up the horses' head gear with gaily coloured plumes, were satisfaction enough in Dougie's estimation. He knew well enough that it was virtually a deadend occupation, but to each his own. The highlight of the dubious career was when the destination was reached.

Mounting the horse at the top of West Nile Street, he would make a whooping headlong dash down the steep cobbled slope with sparks spraying from the horse's hooves, stopping all the other traffic and attracting everyone's attention to the Big City Cowboy!

Family Loyalties

Hopeful to me as are the gates of hell,
Is he who, hiding one thing in his heart,
Utters another.

—*Homer* – *"Iliad"*

NOWADAYS ANDY WAS able to wear his new suit more often. In fact he had another, normally reserved for Sunday wear. However, he noticed that there was less pressure by his Mother on him and his brothers to make the compulsory attendances at Sunday school in the Glasgow Cathedral.

Conditions at home were improving. His Father had, at long last, acquired a reasonably well-paid and secure job as a corporation tram conductor and was stationed at Dennistoun Depot. This was a real breakthrough, as any job with the corporation was not to be sneezed at. His Dad loved a uniform. Any uniform!

A few luxuries were becoming more readily available. There were one or two extra suits in the wardrobe. Andy and his brother collected a roll of bright floral waxcloth from Bow's in the High Street, for the kitchen. His uncle, an unemployed painter, was paid to whitewash the ceiling and hang the few rolls of wallpaper, speckled with red and yellow roses.

However, Andy still worked the paper run. His Mother still scrubbed the classroom floors, and his Father had never once produced an unopened pay packet! The local boozing shops had the priority where that was concerned.

It was a Friday and Andy was leaving school and running homewards to prepare for the evening newspaper run. He knew that he didn't have a lot of time to spare. However, it was his father's pay day and the food cupboard was pretty bare. From experience his mother was well aware that she would be unlikely to obtain the remnants of the pay poke before ten o'clock that night, and there would probably be a good going rammy before she received the pittance. Andy had some idea what to expect when he saw her leaning out of the raised bedroom window, looking into Rottenrow.

"Andy, son", she called, "I know you have to attend to your papers, but you will have to run round to the 'Cot Bar'."

It was becoming a ritual on a Friday night and his newsagent wasn't at all pleased at regular late arrival especially on such a busy night.

"Tell your Dad to give you enough for a pound of rhubarb jam and a cutting loaf from the store." He retraced his steps and ran like a hare round to the pub at Glebe Street, opposite the Royal.

It was closed. It didn't open till five o'clock. The publican, though, was already assured of his custom. The men were already lounging about the closemouth next door, where the bookie's runner had his lucrative stance, catering for the punters among the walking patients from the Infirmary and from others

41

who had been taking advantage of his "tick" book during the rest of the week. And of course most of the cash was going in one direction only!

His Dad's tall figure stood out from the rest of the bunch at the pub door. After all, his smart dark green, made-to-measure corporation uniform with the shiny brass buttons was a distinguishing mark of progress, and was prominent among the slouching collection of bedraggled suits and down-at-heel boots and shoes. In fact, he towered above the rest and to Andy he seemed quite handsome with the military-like, green baize cap perched rakishly on the back of his head.

Separating from the group he strode haughtily towards Andy while rummaging into his open pay packet. Both he and Andy knew that the damned wages should have been home when he finished his six-till-two shift. He hated like hell being approached in this manner, but had learned to accept it, he vowed to himself that when he did get home he would make bloody sure that it wouldn't happen again in front of his mates. Andy had a fair idea of what his Father was thinking — he had witnessed the outcome often enough after seeing him consume a good bevvy and developing his Dutch courage.

Yet, strangely, Andy couldn't quite suppress a sense of pride in his Dad at this moment. Pride at his brilliant ornate cap badge with the fishes, bell and tree glistening in the evening sunlight.

"Hello, son, just out of school? What did you learn today?"

He had a few jugs in him already. Andy could tell by the red flushing on his cheeks and the beads of sweat on his prominent forehead. Andy reckoned that he had already been for some Eldorado from the licensed grocer in Stirling Road.

"My Ma sent me round, you'll have to give me some money for messages at the Co-op."

His Dad said, "There's still a wee while before the bar opens, son, come on over for a sit down and we'll have a chat, man-to-man."

Andy was worried about the paper run and he was already late. "Listen Dad, I don't suppose that you will be home till late tonight. I have to go now, the newsagent pays me tonight and my Ma will need a few bob before you get back, so I'm off."

"Just a minute, son," he said. They sat on a bench at the Infirmary casualty entrance, normally used for patients and visitors needing a rest.

Andy sensed the line of patter that was coming. He knew his Father had a fancy woman for a start. The attraction was probably the uniform as well as a percentage of his Father's wages, which should be invested in the house. He wouldn't have a girl friend for long if she could see him, shirt tail hanging out, vomiting India Pale Ale into the jaw box and hurling vile dog's abuse at his demented mother on a Saturday night. And he knew the mistress was a divorced tramcar cleaner from Fisher Street.

"Andy, boy, I know you are growing up and beginning to notice things. I realise that I should be a better Father to you and your Ma. I couldn't find a better wife than your Mother in the City of Glasgow."

The usual sickening parrot-like slobbering introduction to more serious matters, he thought. The punch line was coming. He had grown up. He had noticed things.

"I think you seen me with a woman in Duke Street last week, well I. . . ."

This confirmed Andy's suspicions, and he was so bloody angry that he interrupted his Dad's attempt at making excuses.

"Look Da, I know all about it."

His Dad started to fume and bluster with embarrassment.

"I never told Ma, but I followed you and your cow into her flat in Fisher Street!"

Andy didn't really revive till he was halfway down the Street. An old wife selling flowers was asking him if he was all right. As he lay propped up against the Infirmary railing the old wife's face was a dim outline, the din of cartwheels was splitting his skull and Coia's ice cream shop lights were dancing crazily across the street.

"Jesus Christ. What the hell happened!"

His Dad had landed him a full blooded stotter to his left earhole. He felt as though his brains had shot straight through his other ear!

"Well," he thought, "there goes the bread and jam" — and any fatherly affection that he may have had.

When he revived and had collected his evening papers, he noticed that the headlines were screaming about the possibility of war!

Fat black clouds rolled over the Townhead!

43

Holiday Happiness

Man is the artificer of his own happiness.
— *Thoreau*

EVENTS SEEMED to be moving with lightning rapidity. The adolescent is unable to contemplate the possibility that the beauty of life could be obliterated in the finality of existence. Life should go on for ever.

The social environment influences in childhood and youth will, however, initiate the need to bring about changes and improvements in the accepted order of society. Distinctions and divisions are recognised — and recorded for future reference — in the inquisitive mind of early maturity.

Since Andy's Father had become a tram conductor his contribution — meagre as it was — coupled with Andy's regular wage from the newsagent and his Mother's financial management, meant the family found that they could plan a holiday at one of the popular Clyde Coast holiday resorts. Largs, Ayr and Saltcoats were the long-established firm favourites of the working class families of Glasgow. The Toffs from Newton Mearns and Pollokshields usually ventured overseas — to the Isle of Man!

Andy's Mother decided on Saltcoats.

When the coast landlady in Dockhead Street confirmed the accommodation for the last week in August and the first week in September of 1939, of a single bedroom, including the personal use of a gas cooker, Andy and his brother were elated. A break from the newspaper and milk delivery chores and smoke-shrouded Townhead atmosphere! Off to a world of sunshine, lush green gardens and parks, colourful pavilions and stretches of golden sandy beaches lapped by the silvery sparkling waves of the Clyde estuary.

This, truly was the stuff of dreams!

The hectic preparations were as joyous as the thought of the forthcoming holiday. Andy boosted the newspaper sales in the wards of the Infirmary and to the officers in the control room at Duke Street Prison. In his eagerness to increase his own — and the family's income — he developed a sales pitch at the main gates of the Royal at visiting times. He drummed up the

44

chimney sweeping business during the six weeks' summer school break among the local householders, further augmenting the holiday funds. Priorities were observed. Certain long standing habits had to be ruthlessly — if temporarily — discarded. The heavily studded Parish boots, for a start, were not compatible with the sands at Saltcoats!

The Economic Stores at George Street had the finest selection of white-laced sandshoes in the City — and they were the cheapest. With half-inch thick, white ribbed, rubber soles, red and blue canvas uppers, these brightly coloured "sannies" in the brown cardboard box epitomised the essence of the seaside holiday in the mind of the Townhead schoolboy.

Extra washing time was booked at the Steamie where the City grime was scrubbed out of the household clothing. The air of happiness was infectious. Andy's Mother smiled in contentment at the joy that pervaded her family.

Thoughts of Julia with the fiery cascade of red hair gradually diminished in Andy's memory, although he was still unable to comprehend the reason for such a tragedy. He had heard, and read, about the scourge of tuberculosis in the Glasgow tenements, but the incidence of the disease paled into insignificance when he recalled the seemingly futile and senseless destruction of his first love in Ruchill Hospital. At the time the widespread effect of the illness didn't concern him at all. It had hurt him personally and, selfishly or not, this was all that counted. Nevertheless, Julia's death formulated a pattern in his mind which, in time, would influence his attitude towards religion and other factors which would need to be altered.

The great day dawned. An early rise for all, and with both tattered suitcases packed and tied with stout twine — off to the tramcar stop in Duke Street. The holiday mood seemed to be affecting everybody and everything. The normally grimy windows of the Townhead School glinted in the early morning sunshine.

The sombre surface of the pumping station storage tank sparkled and danced with myriads of reflected sunlight, conjuring up the delights soon to be realised on the beach at Saltcoats. Walking down High Street the stark, forbidding walls and barred cell windows of the Prison assumed, momentarily, a fresh, brighter presentation in his mind's eye.

Approaching the Bell-o'-the Brae, at the steepest part of High Street, Andy watched a heavily laden London & North Eastern goods cart struggling up the cobbled slope. The cart was piled too high with crates of beer, whisky and other goods and was probably heading for Cowlairs in Springburn. He had often acted as a carter's boy; usually just for the thrill of being perched on a moving, horse-drawn vehicle.

But his experience convinced him that the sturdy Clydesdale was being badly treated and overworked. Its load was excessive. There should have been a trace horse. With it flaring nostrils belching great gasping snorts of steam and its iron clad hooves slithering erratically over the highly polished cobble stones, Andy sensed trouble!

The hunched-up carter, flaunting a stubby blackened clay pipe in thick boozy lips under the lowered skip of his bunnet, was lashing hell out of the sweaty, soaking flanks of the big beast with the knout of a short, heavy rope.

Andy stopped and watched, fascinated, as his mother insisted that he move on. At this point, Big Tam Chalmers, a well known local hardman, appeared alongside Andy, sprouting a half-smoked Woodbine and stopped to watch the scene with glowering eyebrows. He knew Andy vaguely through his Father.

"He's going to ground that bloody horse, you know," he muttered angrily to Andy.

The carter continued to flay the Clydesdale with even more vicious strokes of the rope and was now standing on his platform lashing out with the reins.

The horse was terror-stricken. It had reached its limit of endurance. Its mouth was wide open, its head drawn ruthlessly upwards and its nostrils were a mass of flecks of foam.

Big Tam could stand it no longer — and promptly lost his head! While having no knowledge whatsoever of the carter's nationality — or religion — he lurched towards the offending creature like a raging bull.

"Durty Fenian bastard," he roared, "lay off the fucking horse!" Whereupon he made a flying leap on to the footboard and booted the startled carter on to the street. The carter landed on his arse right in front of the Springburn tramcar.

Pandemonium reigned!

The tram guard mechanism scooped up the dishevelled carter and he disappeared under the bodywork, screaming blue murder. The scene was enveloped in a mass of bright blue sparks as the driver applied the emergency brake blocks on the silver lines.

Big Tam grabbed the reins. Leaning over precariously from the footboard, he made a vain attempt to soothe the panic-stricken Clydesdale by slapping its soaking buttocks. The horse responded by unceremoniously skelping Tam across the kisser with its shaggy tail!

He wasn't at all pleased at the turn of events and the horse's undignified reaction! And the Clydesdale was hardly overjoyed at the treatment being meted out on its flanks!

A crowd gathered. To the kids it resembled a Wild West scene. Big Tam was beginning to sense that he was becoming the centre of ridicule. His response to the catcalls was as expected.

"Away and bile yer bloody hieds: I'll soon square this bastard."

The horse, embittered by the extra-heavy load, the abuse being heaped on its exhausted body, and the general commotion, reared its tail to the vertical position and directed an ear splitting explosive fart into Tam's face!

The force of the frightful fart whipped Tam off his perch and he couped headlong into the street between the front wheels of the stationary cart! And the horse wasn't finished. As Tam lay in a crumpled heap, the Clydesdale completed its toilet, enveloping Big Tam in great brown globules of hot stinking shit and directing a well-aimed stream of hot steaming piss into his cursing mouth.

"Jesus Christ!" Andy shouted, tears of ecstasy streaming down his cheeks, "did you ever see anything so funny in your life, Maw?"

Andy's "Maw" belted him across the earhole!

"You watch your bloody language in the main street in front of all these people, I'm fair affronted," she chided.

The womanfolk were appalled at the whole disgusting affair. The big fat traffic cop in his white coat, disgruntled at the long line of disrupted traffic, which now stretched all the way to Glasgow Cross, moved up from his stance at George Street, and took control of the situation.

47

"This is a damned disgrace," he addressed all and sundry, "move along and get on with your business." The carter couldn't help. The tram driver had dragged him out from below his vehicle feet first, and had dumped him on the pavement.

Big Tam Chalmers, covered in fresh dung, had crawled into the nearest pend close and was nowhere to be seen.

The cop belted the horse across the arse with his helmet. Its legs gave way and it collapsed in a slithering, snorting heap in the middle of the High Street, trapping one of the cop's big flannel feet.

Andy would willingly have forgone an hour of his holiday to have witnessed the outcome. As it was, they were already late for the Saltcoats train and had to make a hurried exit for the station. Andy supposed they would send for a trace horse and a team of men from the stables in the College goods yard. He knew it was no small problem to raise a fallen Clydesdale which couldn't find a firm footing with which it could right itself!

Saltcoats Sunshine

All human joys are swift of wing,
For heaven doth so allot it;
That when you get an easy thing,
You find you haven't got it!
— *Eugene Field*

THE BEDROOM window of the holiday flat at Saltcoats was situated immediately above Woolworths' Store, and faced on to the narrow part of the town's main thoroughfare — Dockhead Street. A number of wall-fixed, red painted rails projected over the shop front, supporting a galaxy of full blown toy balloons of every hue in the rainbow, all within Andy's easy reach.

Bouncing and swinging in the soft, seaweed-scented summer breeze, the colourful assortment mingled with near life-sized models of Donald Duck and Mickey Mouse, rubber crafts, sand pails and spades, soft toy donkeys, gleaming trumpets and tin whistles, brown scaly crocodiles, and a fluttering profusion of multi-coloured bathing suits and swimming trunks.

Directly opposite, the baker and confectioner displayed a huge variety of tissue papered sticks of rock, inlaid with red lettering proclaiming the delights and attractions of Saltcoats and other Clyde holiday resorts. The appetising whiff of tray-loads of newly baked white and brown bread, sausage rolls, treacle and soda scones drifted upwards and over towards Andy's open window.

Hordes of happy, holiday-hungry, bantering mothers and fathers jostled in the narrow street with uncontrollable, screaming, boisterous children. There were short, fat, semi-clad working men with bulging beer bellies, supported by fully extended brown belts or braces and tall, skinny, matchstick men with deeply serrated rib cages, ridiculously thin legs knobbly knees topped with wide flaring shorts.

Most of the men sported brand new tartan or virgin white bunnets protecting balding pates from the hot midday sun. Big busty, broad-beamed, blustering mothers hurled veiled threats at their raucous offspring.

The kids pranced around with city-white topless torsos, already turning pink in the blistering heat.

The noisy and picturesque panorama of Dockhead Street from the bedroom window accurately reflected an abrupt change from the humdrum monotony of smoke-laden work-shops and moulding sheds, the constant clamouring of the ship-yards upriver, and the menial daily tasks of the toil-worn house-wife. The vast expanse of golden sandy beach was peppered with candy-striped deck chairs supported on rickety wooden struts. Beach balls and triangular kites drifted in the sea breeze.

A passing, pulsating paddle steamer capsized the shore-line rubber rafts with its heavy undulating wave effect, producing pretentious, piercing laughter from the overturned occupants. Bright yellow Italian ice-cream carts were dotted along the flower-fringed esplanade dispersing gallons of vanilla and strawberry streaked wafers and monster cones.

A sweating group of sombrely-clad trumpet, trombone and euphonium players from the Salvation Army were surrounded by a circle of near-naked children and solemn-faced parents, enthusiastically supporting a rendering of "All Things Bright and Beautiful, the Lord God made them All".

Andy would contemplate whether the Lord God could be

responsible for the less attractive creations in society? If one, why not the other? After all the preacher was proclaiming the Lord's limitless control of everything.

At sunset, Mrs White, the stout landlady with the floral apron, would invite Andy's mother into the spacious living-room for a session of women's chat over tea and biscuits, leaving Andy and his brother to argue over the events of the day. Mrs White had the most ornate H.M.V. wireless set that Andy had ever seen. The radio, rich dark brown and highly polished, with finely woven loudspeaker panels, was semi-circular and topped with a gold crest portraying a dog listening intently at the fluted megaphone of a spring-wound gramophone.

Mounted in the centre of her glass-topped dressing table, and surrounded by a selection of daintily frilled silk doilies, Andy concluded that Mrs White was a lady who had a bob or two!

Being the eldest, Andy would on occasions be invited to "sit quietly" and indulge in the pleasures of Mrs White's palatial living room, and her fascinating wireless set! He was absorbed in a discussion by two political commentators on the ethics — or otherwise — of an aerial attack on a town in Spain during the Spanish Civil War.

The town, Guernica, had been razed to the ground. It had been almost completely obliterated in a bombardment from Focke-Wolfe dive bombers that had been dispatched in squadrons from airfields in Fascist Italy and Nazi Germany. According to the discussion, the significance of the horrific event seemed to have been that such a tremendous loss of life and level of destruction could have been achieved in a raid of such short duration. Spanish Royalist sources justified the attack on the grounds that the bomber pilots were rehearsing and practising this new concept of warfare. Guernica was, anyway, a hotbed of Red Republicans!

A rehearsal? Could it be that Harry McShane and Jimmy Maxton were, after all, correct in their assessment of the war in Spain? He had heard Big Peter Kerrigan haranguing the crowd at a street corner political meeting at Cathedral Square, just before coming to Saltcoats. Andy hadn't paid much attention at the time. He had remained on the fringe of the listeners. It was for adults anyway.

On the other hand Kerrigan would know more about it than

the armchair radio commentators. Kerrigan, he knew, had been there! He had been in the thick of the struggle with the British Battalion and had predicted that the destruction of Guernica and other atrocities signalled the prelude to a European conflagration.

And so it proved to be! Indeed, it became World War II.

Following on the unprovoked expansionist invasions of Czechoslovakia and Poland, Mrs White called on Andy and his Mother to hear the Special Announcement by Mr Chamberlain on the Government's decision to declare war against Germany.

The Scottish News reader on the six o'clock bulletin spoke ominously of hurried arrangements for the mass distribution of gas masks, and preparations for the immediate evacuation of women and children from the cities and other densely populated areas. The "rehearsal" seemed to have finished.

The Warmongers were on the march!

The family's holiday of a lifetime had been ruthlessly severed by the scalpel of war, panic packing and the mad rush for home, although time would confirm that there had been no real necessity for the emergency measures to be introduced at that particular period. The ghastly gas masks were duly allocated and mass evacuation to less vulnerable areas of the country was undertaken — but was optional.

Andy's family decided against it, for the time being at any rate, at least until the air raids started. Andy's grandparents, who lived in Stranraer, had extended an invitation to the family if things hotted up in Glasgow.

The Emergency

As long as war is regarded as wicked, it will always have its fascination. When it is looked upon as vulgar, it will cease to be popular. — *Wilde*

TOWNHEAD was in turmoil.

The Territorial Army was preparing itself, as the British Expeditionary Force, for France. Conscription was the order of the day. Tribunals were invoked to establish the qualifications of applicants who felt that they merited the status of essential, reserved occupations — in the munitions industry and related branches of the economy.

Other, more vigorous, investigative committees were introduced for the examination of conscientious objectors! Some men decided, in their own minds, and as a matter of principle, against the indignity of trial by the C.O. tribunals — and suffered the consequences.

Eligible single women were drafted into the Women's Land Army. Others occupied the vacancies in the Corporation Transport Department, the factories and shipyards, created by the conscription of the young men. Hundreds of thousands were directed into war weapons production at Royal Ordnance Factories in Hillington and Bishopton.

But a powerful swell of movement opposed to war developed. Some of these men were pacifists. Others were radically against the particular nature and origins of the current war.

When Andy got back home from Saltcoats the popular street song indicated the feeling that existed in the minds of the people.

> VOTE, VOTE, VOTE FOR ABYSSINIA,
> WE'LL HAVE THE FASCISTS ON THE RUN,
> YES, BUY A PENNY GUN — SHOOT MUSSO UP THE
>   BUM!
> AND WE'LL NEVER SEE THE FASCISTS ANY MORE!

Bob Cooney, McCormack, Jimmy Fleming and Peter Kerrigan had survived the war in Spain and had returned to continue the struggle in the Townhead and in the Gorbals. However, a number of Glasgow members of the International Brigade hadn't come back.

Guy Aldred, who described himself as a "Non Parliamentarian Communist" and a staunch supporter of the principles expounded by the socialist John Maclean, operated his press and propaganda machine from the Strickland Press premises, halfway along George Street. His shop window illustrated horrifying gory photographs of mutilated men from the First World War as a portent of things to come.

Currently beating the pacifist drum, Guy Aldred wielded a

vitriolic pen, and, with his shoulder length hair and quaint baggy knickerbockers, was one of the most capable orators in the Townhead.

His political pronouncements were powerful! He was radically opposed to the violence and horror of war, and directed the blame for war, in any form of society, to the State apparatus. War, he said, is an expression of State power where the motive is profit.

His theories on how to prevent or curtail all forms of modern warfare seemed, on the face of it, to be simplicity itself. He advocated that all workers throughout the world engaged in the manufacture and production of weapons of war-related equipment — uniforms and stores — should down tools at once, in an international wave of protest.

Furthermore, all existing stocks of war potential should be ruthlessly destroyed. War, in any form, or under any pretence, could not then be initiated. And that was it!

Aldred's theory and his most significant slogan, "Down with all War", were diametrically opposed to the principle and theories of men like Peter Kerrigan and Harry McShane — the two Gorbals stalwarts — who proclaimed the justification of war in certain circumstances. Although they and their associates coincided with Aldred's belief in profit and capital as the motivating factor, they were convinced of the need for opposing Fascism through the use of arms, whatever form it might assume, and wherever it reared its ugly head.

A Political Apprenticeship

The world is my country, all mankind are my brethren, and to do good is my religion.   — *Thomas Paine*

THE BASEMENT area of the south block of Cathedral Court included a Corporation public hall. Andy's Aunt Agnes was the hall caretaker and keyholder.

Since his aunt had become virtually housebound due to the paralysing effects of arthritis, Andy had assumed the task of opening and preparing the premises for the numerous organisations which had registered bookings for meetings and concerts, and Band of Hope lectures and film shows. The whole spectrum of political and religious thought represented in the Townhead took advantage of the ideal facilities that were available in the public hall.

The Gospel Singers, the Secular Society, Co-operative Women's Guild, the Rechabites, Labour Party, Freethinkers, Alcoholics Anonymous and the Independent Labour Party all booked sessions at regular intervals. Andy, a regular witness to such a galaxy of experienced and convincing orators, and occasionally becoming involved in fringe discussion, acquired an early political consciousness and training.

He was nearly sixteen years old. Already, he was expressing a keen interest in the activities of the City Central Branch of the Young Communist League and developed friendships with some of the young members of the Independent Labour Party. His Aunt Agnes, who was a member of the I.L.P., encouraged his association with the latter, but strongly advised him against his connections with the "extremist elements" in the Y.C.L.

Initially, he was attracted to the social and sporting aspect of the Young Communist League. A keen cyclist, Andy often joined the road touring group of the Y.C.L., who, in turn, had close ties with the Clarion Cycling Clubs. Most of the young members took part in camping expeditions, or, through the facilities of the Scottish Youth Hostels Association, organised week-end tours to certain Scottish Youth Hostels in the country, where the social activities were integrated with lively and radical political debate.

At about this time Andy's Uncle Willie (his Mother's brother) had managed to find a position for him as an apprentice electrical fitter. Uncle Willie was an engineer with the Clyde Valley Electrical Power Company. The first year apprentices' wage rate was lamentable in this, as yet, unorganised industry. Trade unionism was noticeably thin on the ground in the electricity supply industry at this time. Certainly Andy found it quite impossible to retain anything of his miserable wage packet as pocket money. In fact, a ten journey ticket from St Enoch railway station, based on a five day working week, almost killed his wages stone dead, and, by the time he had carried a daily piece to his work, the bloody mockery of an income was well nigh exhausted!

As for his Mother, she received practically damn all! He was able, for a time, to continue the newspaper delivery run, and the proceeds from this, coupled with a few bob from his Aunt Agnes, as hall convener, proved sufficient to buy a few basic tools from the stalls in "The Barras", and a couple of sets of brown boiler suits.

The fact of being employed at all — and in a skilled trade — dressed in the brand new boiler suit with shiny chrome-plated buttons, imbued him with a sense of pride, and a degree of independence.

His "political apprenticeship", obtained in the public hall at Cathedral Court, and his connections with the youth of the Y.C.L. and I.L.P., very soon came to the forefront. He became embroiled in the surging trade union movement, and was subsequently elected as a member of the Clydeside engineers' apprentices' committee.

Unprovoked Assault!

Ignorance never settles a question.
— *Disraeli*

IN FAIRNESS to the Corporation halls letting committee, there was no discrimination exercised in its policy of allocation to potential clients. Actually, the decision to accept or reject an application was virtually controlled by Aunt Agnes. When general policy of letting was being discussed, the police committee, on the recommendation of the Chief Constable and the senior officials of the Criminal Investigation Department, frowned on certain applications and opposed their acceptance.

In particular, the emergency powers section of the C.I.D., concerned about reports of foreign, subversive infiltration, objected bitterly to certain proscribed organisations, whose aims and policies, they maintained, constituted a grave menace to society.

Sillars, the Chief Constable, summed up the serious situation when addressing the halls committee. " My men have more than enough on their plates in contending with the known subversive organisations, without having to deal with the activities of so called respectable 'front' groups, meeting in the hole and corner, underground halls and premises that your committee controls." The Chief Constable, however, had no power of veto, so his suggestions were generally dumped!

It was a chilly Saturday night in November. A group of about ten men and women — described in Aunt Agnes' book as "The Friends of Ireland" — assembled at the alloted time, around seven o'clock.

Earlier in the evening, Andy had accepted the delivery of a crate of twelve bottles of Guinness. This, of course, was not uncommon among the various groups who frequented the premises, although Aunt Agnes was quite strict in her precautions against the import of anything stronger.

The meeting having been opened for business by the chairman, Andy, pottering around in the detached small kitchen, was only vaguely aware of the statements being made by the speakers from the raised platform in the main hall.

Andy was quite unconcerned as to the general theme of the meeting and the discussion was, in the main, incoherent, except when raised voices made reference to "Sinn Fein", and to the "Ancient Order of Hibernians".

An interval was called for at eight-fifteen and Andy duly supplied the highly polished, half-pint beer measures to the thirsty participants. The women of the company produced sandwiches and filled up the big teapot from Andy's boiling water urn. He cleared up the overflowing ashtrays in the main hall, cleaned and replaced them, while mumbled conversation continued between the few who chose to remain in the kitchen area.

Aunt Agnes was able to make a random inspection during the break to ensure that all was as it should be, and no rowdiness. She left before the meeting resumed satisfied that everything was in order. Andy and one of the men helped her up the steep flight of stairs. With the time-honoured vote of thanks to the Chair the meeting finished at ten-fifteen. It seemed to have been successful.

Andy was thanked for his services in providing comfortable

heating, good lighting, excellent kitchen and catering facilities — and was awarded a five bob tip from the lady in charge after she called for a whip round. On a whole, the company had shown themselves to be a well-mannered bunch, had used the ashtrays and had returned the beer measures. And they had obviously appreciated Andy's efforts!

He cleaned up the kitchen, brushed out the floor and platform of the main hall, assembled the chairs in orderly ranks, then collected a dozen empty Guinness bottles which he stored in the kitchen cupboard. The empties would be returned to the "Cross Keys" in Rottenrow — a fairly profitable night's work, he concluded.

He closed off the gas supply to the cooker, and, after a cursory glance around the kitchen and hall, switched off the lights.

The group had gone.

Locking the lower doors, he headed towards the steep and curving flight of dull carpeted stairs which led to the main, upper door, at the Cathedral Court level.

The stairway was dimly lit by a brown dirty, fly-speckled forty-watt bulb that was controlled from the main upper door. It was suspended high up in the apex of the staircase. Glancing up, he realised that the lamp would have to be changed soon, but he didn't know how the hell he would ever reach it. It must have been inserted when they made the buildings, he thought.

He overheard a muted voice and assumed that one or two members of the company had loitered behind for an extended debate — not at all unusual, but the conversations usually continued in the upper backcourt.

Climbing the first few steps, he was confronted by two men crouching on their hunkers in the recess in the curve of the staircase.

He was momentarily taken back. His initial thought was that two of the group had returned on some business or other — perhaps to make a further booking of the premises. One thing was certain, they shouldn't have been where they were at that time.

Both men were unshaven and wore shin length, dirty black and bedraggled overcoats, topped by yellowing white mufflers. He soon realised, even in the poor illumination, that they had not formed part of the departed company.

Each of them were topped with the all too familiar, greasy,

broad skipped bunnet with the loosened snap catch, so that the eyes were hooded by the lowered skip. Big Kerrigan would have described them, politically, as members of the lumpen proletariat.

Andy immediately recognised the pair of them as a couple of bloody hooligans who were up to no good — and he instantly went on the defensive. Did they think he was a straggling member of the group who had just left? Or did they know him personally?

But he had no time for any further thoughts on the matter. They both pounced!

Andy, still in his brown boiler suit, automatically reached into his narrow three-feet-rule pocket, where he normally carried the new, bakelite handled, six-inch screwdriver. It had slipped downwards, though, and all he was able to grab in the few seconds available was the useless Rabone rule.

The man nearest to Andy was, by now, removing his bunnet, and in the first few seconds he recognised the tell-tale glint of the blade of a cut throat razor expertly stitched and embedded into the sharp skip of the flashing bunnet.

Andy, at a lower level, was at a distinct disadvantage. He ducked, instantaneously, before the lunging man struck him on the legs with his head and his assailant, overbalanced, hurtled head over heels to the bottom of the lower stairs, while both men were screaming, at the top of their voices. "Irish bastard!"

At precisely the same moment his mate produced an empty beer bottle from the depths of his coat pocket.

The man who had catapulted downstairs was now righting himself, and, although obviously dazed by the fall, was staggering upwards towards Andy's back.

The upper man, mouthing vile sectarian abuse, aimed a vicious kick with his heavily booted right foot. It struck Andy on the left shoulder with the force of an express train! His left arm and side were completely paralysed.

The lower man booted him on the ball of his right leg, while trying for a stranglehold round his neck. Andy was forced to his knees. The crouching action spilled the rule out of his elongated pocket and brought the screwdriver into the grasp of his right hand.

He plunged it, indiscriminately, into the body of his bottle swinging opponent! The bottle struck, and the blade penetrated simultaneously!

A final crippling, booted kick into his groin and Andy knew nothing more as he leapt into a deep black pit of unconsciousness.

Revival – and Revenge?

In taking revenge, a man is but equal to his enemy, but in passing it over he is superior.　　　　— *Bacon*

ANDY MADE a pain searing, temporary revival two hours later, in the casualty ward of the Royal Infirmary. As the confused state of consciousness returned, his immediate reaction was that he had been blinded. There was a scorching, singeing pain in his eye sockets. Surely they hadn't done *that* with the razor?

Had he lost his sight?

He soon realised that his entire face and skull had been enveloped in swathes of broad bandages. A strangulating elastic binder secured two broken ribs in his chest, while a plaster cast moulding had immobilised his left shoulder with a grip like a vice. Boyd the Blacksmith's steam hammer was pounding relentlessly in his head.

But a sudden surge of excruciating agony from between his legs forced a wild uncontrollable scream from his bruised and swollen lips. The well directed kick by one or the other — perhaps both of the men — had smashed into his testicles! The crashing beer bottle had finished him off.

The pain was insufferable. The doctor hurriedly injected his forearm with a quick action drug. He lapsed again into oblivion.

His Aunt Agnes and his Mother, concerned at the delay — and worried about the keys of the hall! — had found him lying in a pool of blood, an hour after the incident. Fortunately, the Royal was only five minutes away. When he finally came round the following day, and with the bandages partially removed, his Mother — and two policemen — were at his bedside.

"Can you make a statement? Do you remember stabbing

59

Robert Montgomery with a screwdriver? And if so why?"

Andy could hardly believe it!

"Are you normally in the habit of carrying a dangerous weapon?"

"This was some grilling," he thought.

"I can hardly open my bloody gob," he muttered.

"Are my eyes O.K.?" he queried.

He was assured by the nurse that they were.

Montgomery, he was informed by one of the policemen, was in an upper ward, suffering from a severely ruptured spleen and was in an extremely dangerous condition.

The police, quoting the medical report on Montgomery, stated that if he had not been uplifted at the time in question, then it was unlikely that he would have survived.

It occurred to Andy that this bugger Montgomery must be in a helluva state, as he himself felt as though he had been wound through a clothes drying mangle!

At any rate, his immediate reactions and his speech were practically incoherent and, confused with the sharp pains from his lower belly and the pounding thunderclaps in his head, the only response he could muster up was, "Fuck Montgomery!"

His Mother, while sympathetic, wasn't too pleased — neither were the cops — who duly noted it down!

The resulting series of tests, X-rays, injections and, most painful of all, the manipulations to his balls and groin seemed endless.

It was evident from what the cops were saying that Montgomery's mate had not been traced. In fact as far as they were concerned, there hadn't been a third party!

On being discharged after thirteen days with the aid of a walking stick, he was issued with an out patients' report card — and was visited at home by staff from the Criminal Investigation Department.

To Andy, it hardly seemed credible. He had told them all he was able to remember while still in the Royal. His Mother was appalled that her family should even remotely be the concern of the police. The thorough, investigative direction of the questioning, with barely concealed political overtones, left Andy with the distinct impression that the responsibility for the whole diabolical affair was directly attributable to himself.

A prominent Glasgow newspaper, commenting on the situation said, in its editorial column:

This "Friends of Ireland" organisation has been exposed in its true colours and is obviously an active, Glasgow-based faction of the Irish Republican Army.

This incident has demonstrated clearly, that the comments made by Chief Constable Sillars — and quoted in the columns of this newspaper a short time ago — were absolutely correct. We concur with the Chief Constable and demand that tighter controls are exerted in the allocation of meeting and conference facilities by the Corporation's Halls Letting Committee.

Concluding on the theme, and obviously exploiting the current anti-German sympathies generated by the war, the paper summed up, "Furthermore, it should not surprise anyone but the most naive that these terrorists are on the payroll of the German Government."

Andy's wayward, but generally well disciplined — even Christian — home life, allied to his recent political maturing in the socialist tradition had conditioned his mind and attitude into channels of respect for his fellow members of the working class. His mind, his heart, and his body, had been mercilessly assaulted. Would this call for a change in his admiration for the lofty traditions of John Maclean and others whose concepts of "never losing faith in your fellow men" had moulded his aspirations?

The Thinker

ALAN BUCHANAN, two or three years older than Andy, had, for as long as he could remember, been a complete loner, and was inclined to be morose. He had never shown any inclination to become involved in the pranks, fun and frolics, all of which formed an essential fabric of everyday life for the kids of the Townhead School. Alan had been an average scholar during his term and, if anything, expressed a keen interest in the study of English literature and recent history. While in the advanced (secondary) division of his term he was forever immersed in the intensive study of books and pamphlets in a secluded corner of the school shed during the morning and afternoon intervals. Most of his reading material had not been issued by the education authority.

He seemed completely oblivious to the shrill exaggerated screams and cries of his schoolmates, busily engaged in varying degrees of minor warfare on the flagstoned playground. Although he lived in nearby Stanhope Street, he had never been known to join in the blood-curdling roars of the ring of observers in Collins Street, where the almost daily session of fisticuffs took place at four o'clock.

He carefully avoided trouble with his mates, and was never likely to become a participant in after-school fights. After school, he was always seen to be heading in the general direction of upper Castle Street, presumably to the Townhead public library, opposite Parliamentary Road.

Alan was tall and powerfully built for his age group and had a thick crop of jet black curly hair. His eyes were as black as coal, and, to Andy were completely unfathomable. Andy (in his own opinion) was an extrovert, and fancied his chances as a fair judge of character. Yet he had never been able to plumb the depths of mystery surrounding Alan Buchanan.

Perhaps it was the eyes. They were almost hypnotic, Andy thought. It was quite unknown for Alan to have demonstrated openly any form of interest or affection towards anyone else during his two year period of senior school training. It was therefore surprising, and almost a contradiction, that an affinity should have been struck between he and Andy when they had left school and started work.

Alan had started as an assistant in a well-known gents' outfitters in Gordon Street. He could never accept that it was quite his scene, and hated every minute of his working day.

The Introduction

Do you think that revolutions are made
with rose water?   — *Chamfort*

IT HAD LONG been established tradition in the big industrial
centres for the young — and not so young — men to take up
selected stances at the street corners. And so it was in the
Townhead.

If unemployed, then they could stand all day long. If
working, then, after tea, the assembled groups would meet and
discuss the events of the day, the rammies with the gaffer or the
defects of the shop steward. The subject of girls and women
usually monopolised the trend of conversation!

Dougie, Andy and a few others in the "working" group
generally met at the corner of Castle Street and Cathedral
Street. This was convenient to Coia's Café, opposite the Royal,
to which they could adjourn, at intervals, for a plate of hot
peas or the well known Glasgow delicacy — the McCallum.
Occasionally their conversation would be disturbed, and their
attention distracted, by the heavy rumble of the military
convoys which invariably passed this particular location before
turning down into High Street.

The convoys, snaking away into the distant end of Cathedral
Street, mainly consisted of three- and ten-ton personnel carriers
sprouting hundreds of soldiers and their equipment and towing
artillery of every design and calibre. The whole formation often
took an hour and a half to pass any given point.

The military units had earlier converged, with well-oiled
precision, from the various Territorial Army drill halls dotted
around the City at Yorkhill Parade, Taylor Street and
Hawthorn Street, but primarily from the depot of the Highland
Light Infantry stationed at Maryhill Barracks. Civilian traffic
was either stopped or diverted by the military and civilian
police, ensuring free, uninterrupted movement for the convoy.
The same route was used by hundreds of smart, disciplined
marching soldiers fronted by drum beating, bagpipe skirling,
tartan clad bands.

When the men marched by to the beat of a thousand studded

feet, on their way to war, the scene was resplendent with colour and sound and attracted hordes of youthful observers from the drab, uninteresting tenement slums of the surrounding district.

The Awakening

ANDY AND DOUGIE had just returned from having a wee refreshment in Coia's Café and were lounging at the corner. It was a miserable drab Thursday night, around eight o'clock. It was the night before pay day. And they were skint. The fact that it was pissing cats and dogs didn't help.

A passing parade of bedraggled troops, clad in camouflaged rubber ground sheets and heads lowered against the lashing rain, scarcely merited attention.

As the rain got heavier, they were gradually forced back into the doorway of the dilapidated, windowless, converted shop which formed the corner of the two streets. They had never ventured into the place before, preferring to lend their bodily support to the Old Barony Church across the way.

The boys continued their nattering in the vestibule area of the premises. The inner door opened and they fully expected to be hunted for loitering. Instead, they were completely surprised to be confronted by Alan Buchanan.

"Hello lads!" — he seemed to have been momentarily taken aback himself — "come on inside." A girl appeared behind Alan.

"Olga, would you mind collecting a couple of bottles of Tizer and some biscuits from Coia?"

"By the way, it's on me lads, O.K.?" turning to Andy.

The place was absolutely alien to the lads. Andy remembered from his newspaper run, that it had once been a makeshift tea-room, catering for Women's Guilds and the like from the local churches. It had certainly changed since he last made a delivery — as he was soon to notice! Alan ushered them indoors as Olga donned a hood and went to the café.

The place was warm, and they didn't need much coaxing to come in out of the rain. There was a red-hot, pot-bellied stove at the far end, with a flue pipe leading through the rear wall. The first item to attract their attention was a massive red and white linen banner on the main wall which boldly pronounced "MICHAEL BAKUNIN HALL — THE ANARCHIST FEDERATION"

"These are a few of my mates, and you have just met Olga," Alan said, introducing the lads to half a dozen men, mainly quite young, but two of whom were middle-aged, and, in Andy's opinion, foreigners.

The two older men were quite heavily bearded, and subconsciously relating them to the distinctive style and demeanour of Guy Aldred, Andy concluded that they were definitely not locals. Neither were the others, for that matter, but he assumed that they were Glaswegians.

Andy and Dougie noticed that the others didn't seem remotely interested in the pounding boots of the marching soldiers, or the rending squeals of braking and gear-changing vehicles in the convoy, which were deafening when the doors of the hall were opened.

The girl returned with the stuff.

One of the two foreigners locked the doors, and Alan invited the two of them to take a seat on a rickety bench, just inside the door.

"Buchanan seems to be in charge here," Dougie whispered to Andy as they seated themselves in the shoogly pews. Alan moved to a small raised platform, with Olga, and called the company to order.

Dougie, utterly confused was unable to contain himself any longer. He muttered to Andy, between slugs of Tizer, "Listen, they've locked the bloody doors, and we're stuck in here. What's Buchanan up to?"

"What does that mean on the poster? It's no' the Band of Hope, surely? I don't fancy the set-up at all, what do you think?"

Alan had started to speak.

Andy could see that Dougie was ready to start gassing again and whispered: "For Christ's sake, shut your arse and give your mouth a chance. We are in out of the rain, we haven't a halfpenny between us, and you're guzzling a free Tizer. This is better than any Band of Hope. Shut your trap for a minute and we'll see what's happening."

"These hundreds of men passing here," Alan stated, pointing to the doorway, "are workers in uniform. The vast majority have been conscripted into the military machine and their wishes have not been considered. Those who volunteered their services did so because the misery and degradation of unemployment offered no hope whatsoever to themselves and their families." Alan glanced towards Andy and Dougie. "These two lads, Andy and Dougie, were schoolmates of mine. Fortunately — or otherwise — they are currently enjoying the doubtful pleasure of being duly registered wage-slaves of Society — they are working."

Dougie was aghast. He leapt out of his seat.

"Who's a bloody slave?" he roared. "You watch your patter, Buchanan. Nobody tells me what to do unless I feel like doing it. Anyway, I don't know what the hell this is all about. And I don't know why you locked the fucking doors. I'll leave here any time I fancy it. What about you?" turning to Andy. "Do you want to sit here and listen to this load of shit. He says you're a slave, what do you think of that for bloody cheek!"

The rest of the company glanced round briefly but were unperturbed as though they were immune to such interruptions and criticism.

Alan intervened, raising his hands in an apologetic fashion. "Dougie, I am sorry. I used the expression 'slave' in a purely political context. The wage system is a form of slavery. Perhaps if I say that all of us here — including myself — are wage slaves, then maybe you will have a clearer understanding of the term. By the way, feel free to question, or criticise any of us if we use expressions that you cannot grasp. I apologise for assuming that you both might know what we are about."

Dougie sat down again and, inwardly, enjoyed a sneaking sadistic pleasure in having extracted an open apology from Alan. He relished the feeling as Alan continued.

"I intend no offence whatsoever towards Andy and Dougie. Of course they can leave here at any time. But I would ask that they hear me out — at least until the rain eases off.

"Both of you, and certainly a whole lot of others that I know of, will probably harbour certain fixed opinions as to the role of the Anarchist.

"And I wish to make it quite clear, that, on recollection, my own views on the anarchist were completely distorted. That is, until I decided to inquire.

"The most effective method of rectifying the distortion and misinterpretation is to join the ranks of the Federation.

"I am well aware of the fact that the generally accepted image of the anarchist is that of a deranged and totally insane madman, intent on the destruction of the whole fabric of society. Indeed it has been said of us, that we constitute a far greater menace to society than the Communists. Frankly, I consider such a viewpoint to be complimentary to the Federation.

I would go further on that particular score. There is absolutely no possibility of any form of relationship with the Marxists, Socialists, or any of the other so-called acceptable organisations — not at this stage of the struggle, at any rate.

"This is not to say, however, that we would reject a temporary association — provided that the Anarchist Federation maintained the leading role and controlled any given situation! Consider, for a moment, the manifestos and the theories being advanced by the popular political parties with whom we are well-acquainted, as propagated in the Yellow Press and some 'left-wing organs'."

The raincoat and jacket were removed and cast aside. The place was like a furnace, and, with no apparent ventilation some of the seated men followed suit.

Dougie was becoming agitated.

Alan, more comfortable in his shirt sleeves, carried on, "At the present time, the Labour Party may fairly be described as the main working class party advocating policies which have a mass appeal.

"Of course, the Labour Party is wrong, and the people have been duped and misguided all along.

"It is wrong in that it proposes to *alter* the system of Government. It is *reformist* in character — and capitalism cannot be reformed.

"Furthermore, their differences with the Independent Labour Party are in the interpretation of fundamentally similar policies. They coincide, in the long term, in that they also seek reformism.

"Therefore they are also wrong.

"Some of our own comrades, apart from better-known men like Maclean, Gallacher and Shinwell, refused to comply with the system — refused to be compromised — and were jailed as traitors. Traitors to whom?" he shouted.

This was an Alan Buchanan whom neither Dougie or Andy recognised. They had never seen him without the tightly belted raincoat which had been discarded. His arms were gesticulating wildly with carelessly rolled-up shirt sleeves.

"Traitors to the Establishment and all that it represents," he uttered, with his thick black hair bobbing with every gesture and his eyes flashing with uninhibited fanaticism.

Andy was impressed.

Dougie was curious.

They had slugged at least one bottle of Tizer apiece, and they were both bursting for a piss!

As far as Andy could see, there was no sign of a cludgie on the premises. Alan seemed to have eased up for the present and was talking to Olga.

Dougie nudged, and murmured to Andy, "Listen, I don't know about you, but I'm badly needing a pee and if I don't get one smartly it will be splashing about this bloody floor and ruin my new strides into the bargain. Find out if there's a shitehouse in here." Andy, as usual, had to take the lead.

He reached forward, tapped the shoulder of the big bearded man who had locked the door and acquainted him with the impending disaster. The man beckoned to Alan Buchanan, who was just about to introduce Olga as the next speaker.

The man spoke to Alan, who merely nodded and shrugged his shoulders, making no comment. He assumed that the lads wanted out — and they couldn't have found a better excuse for doing so.

Dougie, slightly crouched, and with his legs tightly crossed, was ready to let it rip and couldn't get out quickly enough. The "Beard" opened the door for the lads while Alan said that he would see them again.

As Dougie charged desperately towards the opening door, he

smashed headlong into the toppling frame of a big, fat, uniformed copper! It was instantly obvious to everyone that he had been on "listening duty". During the lull in Alan's statement within the hall, he had leaned his enormous weight against the door in his morbid, information seeking curiosity.

His nose bothering, fat frame clattered down like a ton of bricks inside the hall door, his helmet flying off, and performing circles on the floor.

The inevitable happened. Dougie couldn't hold it in any longer and, after the collision, promptly pissed all over the cop's boots and trousers! The cop had been caught in the act; there wasn't a damn thing he could do about it other than splutter about having come in out of the rain!

Even the hardened Anarchists were forced into howls of laughter at the irony of the situation. All of them had been politically active, but none of them could recall having witnessed such a disgusting — and entertaining — demonstration by a representative of law and order. The sworn enemy nabbed in the well-practised act of ear-wigging, lying prostrated on the Federation floor — and being pissed upon!

Such were the circumstances of the initiation of Andy and Dougie into the Anarchist Federation! For, having relieved themselves in the back of the adjoining close in Castle Street, they returned to the meeting. And Alan was well pleased.

They resumed their seats. Dougie's right trouser leg was rapidly becoming as stiff as a board! He stretched his legs outwards while trying to hide the ominous stain that was forming on his new, tan-coloured strides.

Olga had been asked to make a statement, and was busily sorting out her notes. Andy noticed that nobody made any reference to the incident with the nosey copper. They were probably well accustomed to such uninvited interference by the authorities. No doubt he had collected some subversive information in his wee black book. One thing was certain; he would not have included a detailed account of the fact that he had been unceremoniously couped on his big, fat, interfering arse, into an on-going meeting of anarchists!

The Cauldron

A soldier is an anachronism of which we
must get rid. — *George Bernard Shaw*

ALAN INTRODUCED Olga McGill with a resumé of her background and why she had been motivated into joining the ranks
of the Federation.

She seemed to be well-enough acquainted with the other lads
and it looked as though the information was intended for the
benefit of Andy and Dougie.

The whole company, especially Alan, were pleasantly
surprised that Andy and Dougie had returned at all after such an
unorthodox entry. Alan reckoned that they had not returned for
Tizer. This was long gone. He hoped that their interest had been
roused following his opening statement. He vowed to get them
involved.

Olga was the only daughter of Lithuanian parents, although
she had been born in Mossend. Like hundreds of others, her
parents had suffered religious and political pogroms and
extreme poverty in the Baltic States of Latvia, Estonia and
Lithuania.

Large numbers, forced into exile, had sailed to eastern ports
in Scotland — mainly Leith — and had filtered westwards to the
coalfields and steel-making industry in Lanarkshire.

Alan continued, "I think I have said enough. I was pleased to
see Andy and Dougie coming back after such an unusual
incident, and I think you will agree that they are welcome." A
short stamping of feet indicated the audience's concurrence.

"I would propose that Olga here should invite questions on
the current political situation. Further, I think that our two
guests should be given some priority in this, so if either Andy or
Dougie have any queries at all, let them speak their minds and
direct them to Olga."

There was an embarrassing silence. It lasted for over a
minute. The group cast sidelong glances at Andy and Dougie, as
though encouraging them to say their piece.

The "Beard" deliberately turned round in his chair and
stared directly at the lads as if challenging them to break the
awkward silence.

Dougie couldn't stand it any longer, and he certainly wasn't going to be the first to pose a question. He finally turned to Andy, "Right, why don't you ask something? I don't mind telling you that I'm not sure what the hell I've got myself into here, and I am still not sure what they are nattering about. I know one thing — we can't sit here much longer like a pair of bloody stookies!"

Andy didn't seem all that keen to be the one to make the break. Olga, hands on her hips, looked upwards at something in the ceiling. Andy had sized it up. They had both been forced into a corner, not a very enviable position at all, he thought. And, as usual when he was in Dougie's company, it was down to him again.

So Andy made his first positive contribution to the bubbling cauldron of the political whirlpool. He coughed once or twice as Dougie kept digging him in the ribs with his elbow. He had become involved in fringe conversations during intervals with the various groups at the hall in Cathedral Court — but this was a different ball game entirely. At the moment, he was the centre of attraction. He felt that every word would be carefully scrutinised.

"What about Spain?" he finally blurted out. "My Father thinks the whole episode of the Spanish Civil War was a terrible waste of time and of human lives. He reckons that the outcome was a foregone conclusion."

Another pensive silence.

He knew that he was expected to develop the theme a little. No glances. No encouragement at all. In fact, it occurred to him that perhaps he had touched on a sore subject. Maybe Spain was taboo here. The other organisations, especially the Young Communist League, could talk of nothing else. How the hell was he expected to know their thoughts?

He was beginning to feel a little apprehensive, but he carried on. "Well, my old man should know what he is talking about, he had plenty of experience as a soldier in India and other countries." As he said it, he knew that it was pure bravado. He knew bloody well the role his Father had played.

He finished the question. "I read that hundred of men, including Glaswegians, have been killed and crippled in Spain, so I ask you whether you consider it to have been worthwhile?"

Watching them both intently, Andy now got the distinct impression that Alan and Olga actually revelled in the content of his question. Olga nodded to Alan, indicating that she felt capable of dealing with it. Her eyes glowed in anticipation of making the reply. She launched right in.

"Andy, and comrades, Spain is now a firmly-established Fascist dictatorship. This is being confirmed, daily, in the purges, the ruthless quelling of strikers and their families, and the unbridled attacks being made against the miners in Andalusia and the steel workers in the Basque Territory. The tentacles have spread to Central Europe, in Germany, and that is precisely why, at this very moment, the cream of this country's youth is passing these doors on the road to France — and slaughter.

"Andy asked about the Civil War in Spain, and was concerned about the role of the men who went there. The single most important difference then was that *all* of the men from this and other countries were volunteers! However, all of the participants on the side of the Republic *except the Anarchists*, owed allegiance to, and accepted orders from, either home-grown or foreign political parties and leaders. The Lincoln and British Battalions were guided, respectively, by the American and British Communist Parties.

"In the case of the native Spanish Republican Forces, the Popular Front Forces of the Socialist and Communist Parties were in the main the forces responsible for the establishment of the democratic republican Government. And they constituted the majority of forces who took up the defence of the Republic against the Fascists.

"Where the counter-revolution was concerned, the Royalists and Fascists were firmly in the hands of the Throne and the Church.

"The anarchists were well represented, and fought beside the others at some of the most brutal battles in working class history against the common enemy of Franco-Fascism and the hordes from North Africa.

"*The division of loyalties, on the Popular Front side, contributed, to a major degree towards the defeat in Spain!* Now, precisely, in what vital respect do the Anarchists differ from each and every one of the orthodox political parties that I have just mentioned?

72

"The source of real power lies in the State apparatus. The State maintains its inviolability by the use of the military, the judiciary and the police force. It controls the education system, the Press and the various forms of religion.

"Since they are paid, controlled and operated by the State, they cannot conceivably constitute a menace to its existence. A dog doesn't bite the hand that feeds it. Reformist and revolutionary movements have been conceived, lived and died since the inception of the capitalist system. The Socialist and Labour Parties internationally have generally common aims.

"The world Communist movement, irrespective of the ideological friction which now and again surfaces in the international arena, advocate a more militant, revolutionary method of change. This was demonstrated effectively by Lenin and the Bolshevik Party in Russia in 1917.

"All of these organisations, have a single, common denominator. All of them, without exception, call for the *seizure of the State*. Anarchists, throughout the World, on the other hand advocate the *absolute destruction of the State* and all its power."

Alan thanked Olga — and Andy — and concluded by naming the date of the next meeting. On closing up the Bakunin Hall, Alan invited Andy and Dougie to his own place a couple of nights hence.

Home Brew

Tyrants have not yet discovered any chains that can fetter the mind.
— *Colton*

ALAN'S PLACE was a two-up room and kitchen tenement flat in Stanhope Street, with an outside lavatory. The block was pretty dilapidated, even by Townhead standards.

When the lads arrived at eight o'clock, they found that they had the house to themselves as Alan's old lady was attending a Co-operative Women's Guild meeting at Shiloh Hall, round the corner in St James' Road. He produced a couple of screwtops of India Pale Ale from a dingy recess under the kitchen jawbox. He

73

set them up with a pair of cracked Empire Exhibition mugs, souvenirs from Bellahouston Park, while he used a bashed Sunday school tinny.

Seating accommodation was on the top of the set-in bed. A Jacob's biscuit tin lid was provided as a common ashtray. Finally, Alan extracted two paper bound packets of five Woodbines from the arse of one of the wally dogs on his Maw's fireplace. He was pleased that they had come at all.

Comfortably seated, Alan opened up with a political statement. This, he stressed, was an essential ingredient of Anarchist procedure. It was, he said, invaluable in that it provided an accurate record and evaluation of current affairs. In addition, since the presentation of the statement was rotated among the members at properly convened meetings, then it inspired the individual to maintain a high standard of political consciousness.

However, his review, which he covered so rapidly and which analysed so many factors, was too exhaustive for Andy and Dougie to absorb, so that the statement virtually fell on deaf and totally inexperienced ears. At its conclusion they merely nodded knowingly. Alan instantly recognised his mistake. He had assumed too much. He vowed to himself that it wouldn't happen again. He handed each of the lads a rather crudely printed booklet entitled: *The Role of Anarchism in the World Situation.*

"This will all be new to you," he said, "but meetings like this are taking place all over Europe and the Americas at the present time. And this includes Germany, Italy and Spain, although in circumstances that are less tolerant.

"Anarchists are opposed to the type of war that is currently being fought, since, in this instance the war was instigated by the State, whatever its political persuasion.

"The human being, man, is a living entity — he is absolute reality — an individual.

"Government, the State, is not live. It is completely abstract and purely artificial.

"Therefore the Individual — Man — is superior to the State. This is the crux of the matter, lads.

"But you may wonder why the State can manipulate superior man into participating in the obscenity of war. Why, you may ask, should a situation arise where a fitter, a fishmonger or a tram conductor from the Townhead be forced to don a killer's uniform and be instructed in the most efficient methods of destroying his opposite number in Germany or Italy? After all, the German fitter and the Italian tram conductor are superior *as men* to the German and Italian State apparatus. It is precisely because of the fact that the State can coerce the individual into conducting violent war that Anarchists speak and act as they do.

"*Man loses his identity in war and the Anarchists intend to change this state of affairs.* Furthermore, the Anarchist will pull no punches, observe no rules, in bringing about the change! The State writes the rule book.

"The Anarchists reject these rules out of hand.

"Never under-estimate the cunning of the State. The State is superbly organised. The State, a parasite, will employ any of its many facets, ruthlessly, in its consolidation.

"For example, it will exploit Religion. Trainer killers in the officer level will be adorned with the religious white dog-collar of a padre or a priest as an instrument for the promotion of false piety and righteousness of the cause. Of course there are Spanish, German and Italian priests in their armies.

"Having been expertly conditioned, as workers, in the various form of religion, then these workers as conscripted killers will be induced into making the 'supreme sacrifice' since it is ordained by God! A similar sacrifice will be demanded by the German and Spanish God! They speak a different language — but their Gods demand the same retribution!

"The Vatican has officially recognised the Fascist Government in Rome. The centre of World Christianity has accepted an Ambassador from the Government that was responsible for the murderous attack on the illiterate and defenceless natives of Abyssinia and the people of Spain.

"As for our side, the State sculptor is at this moment preparing a tablet for your fathers and brothers whose names will be inscribed as having fought for 'God, King and Country!'

An Open Forum

The object of oratory is not truth, but
persuasion.   — *Macaulay*

ANDY and Dougie had been encouraged to read. Andy became
an avid reader of Marx, Trotsky, Jack London and works by
Michael Bakunin and Kropotkin. Dougie was less studious but
was currently having a go at Lenin's *State and Revolution*. He
found it to be rather heavy going. But it was he who summed up
their current level of political maturity:

"You know, Andy," he said, "I would never have believed
that I could be persuaded into becoming a political animal. All
that has been said by Alan and the others has come to fruition.
Look at Dunkirk! The more I hear and read of people being
slaughtered and crippled or languishing in concentration camps
for the crime of opposing war, or demanding their basic
freedoms, the more convinced I am that we should be playing a
more active role in the Federation."

Alan and Andy had noticed that Dougie was even developing
a political vocabulary!

Andy took Dougie's comments to heart and duly proposed
that his ideas be translated into action, by recommending that
an outdoor public meeting should be arranged for the following
Sunday. The venue would be at Hutcheson Street, off the
Trongate, which would be comparatively traffic-free on a
Sunday. Alan and Olga would be the principal speakers. Andy
and Dougie accepted that they hadn't yet served enough time in
their political apprenticeships to take on the role of public
speakers. As an introduction though, Andy agreed to be
chairman. Dougie handled propaganda.

Two thousand leaflets were printed in bold red letters and
obtained from a printer in Port Dundas.

The whole group was involved in their distribution, and in
the circulation of sympathetic literature from the Strickland
Press in George Street.

Still, Dougie insisted that the meeting was not yet properly
publicised. Andy acquired a couple of cans of white paint and,
through Dougie, initiated a widespread programme of street

slogans and advertising. Practically every non-cobbled, smooth surfaced street in the immediate vicinity was emblazoned with an appropriate anti-war slogan, coupled with the time and date of the forthcoming meeting.

Dougie organised a look-out system for this aspect of propaganda, and it was carried through after midnight, since it was an offence to deface the street surfaces with paint. But it paid off. The freshly painted slogans attracted the attention of the workers in the morning rush hours. As Alan said, a properly thought-out, short sharp slogan was a powerful medium and generated an immediate interest in the subject.

The slogging, stair-climbing distribution of leaflets and the night-shift sessions of street sloganising were suitably rewarded by a massive turn out at the meeting on a clear, sunny Sunday. When it came to the crunch, Andy was hesitant about making the necessary introductions when confronted with such a multitude. Alan forced the issue. He had to make a start some time. Once in position, he found it to be surprisingly easy.

Alan maintained his usual high standard of oratory and soon warmed to his subject before an audience of at least two hundred and fifty people.

He described, briefly, the origins of the movement and the functions of the Anarchist. His emphasis on the inherent goodness in men found sympathetic reception. The evils that men perpetrated on their fellow-men were the direct result of their influences exerted on their minds, from childhood, by the State.

"The State is a cancer. The malignancy must be exterminated. We Anarchists are constantly vilified in the Press and on the radio as destroyers of society and intent on creating chaos. Can you possibly imagine a more chaotic state of affairs than that which exists in Europe at the present time, where trades unionists, Jews, gypsies and all manner of freedom fighters are being butchered in concentration camps, and this in the interest of maintaining an orderly system of society! The finger of accusation cannot by any stretch of the imagination, be directed at the Anarchists. There is nowhere in Europe where they are in a position to influence events — as yet.

"The war is being described as anti-Fascist. At the moment,

the war is a capitalist war. It is being conducted by two clearly defined groups of power and profit-seeking capitalist systems. And you can be assured that it will not be restricted to Europe. An irreparable crack has appeared in the pattern of world capitalism.

"The workers and peasants of Russia have smashed feudalism and developing capitalism, and have leapt forward to create the basis of a Socialist order in the U.S.S.R. And this is anathema to the contending factions in the war. Irrespective of the outcome, it is absolutely inevitable that the capitalist powers will unite in a holy war against Socialism and Communism in Russia, since the march of Socialism constitutes the *real* menace to the capitalist order.

"We Anarchists are opposed to the conduct of this war. We call upon the workers at Parkhead Forge, Bishopston and all other ordnance factories to stop your machines, to cease the manufacture of all weapons of war and to demand 'no more war'! If the facilities are not available, then it cannot be continued. I ask you all to bear in mind that there is always a worker at both ends of the bayonet!"

Alan's statement seemed to have been well enough received. There were the usual cries from the fringe: "Away and fight," or "Go and join the bloody army, conchie bastards!"

Andy stepped up on to the small portable platform to introduce Olga as the next speaker.

A drunk kilted soldier at the outer edge of the crowd, being supported unsteadily by a gaudily dressed lady of obviously ill-repute, had been heckling intermittently for some time between swigs of booze from his sporran.

As Olga made her opening remarks, the soldier made a head-long breenge into the tightly-packed audience, shouting "Bolshie bastards" at the top of his voice. Some of the bystanders were scattered asunder with his wildly flailing arms as he directed his mad rush towards Olga and the platform. Dougie and Andy confronted him in a vain attempt at defence. The drunk pressed home his attack remorselessly. They were ruthlessly cast aside. Finally, on reaching the base of the flimsy platform, the "Beard" stepped in. He grabbed the soldier. The soldier lashed out viciously with his heavily studded army boots.

The "Beard" expressed an oath of displeasure and promptly applied a firm head-lock with his bulging biceps.

Stumbling, they both lurched heavily against the platform. The combined weight of the interlocked men couped the stand — and its occupant! Olga, launched into space, perfected a decidedly unfeminine dive and crash-landed on the voluptuous bosom of a well-proportioned lady who had been standing placidly on the inner circle of the crowd. The stout lady collapsed into the angered audience, squealing like a banshee! Her enormous proportions, toppling backwards into the tightly packed crowd, produced a domino effect on the predominantly male audience.

A wee skinny man, busily tinkering with his gold Albert watch in his waistcoat pocket, disappeared completely from the scene, crushed like a jelly under the mountainous flesh of the screaming lady!

Her garter-topped stockings and blubbering thighs were by now exposed to all and sundry, much to her chagrin! A general mêlée ensued, amidst a chorus of curses and oaths. There was a flurry of big new checked Sunday bunnets.

Loud, uncontrolled expressions of anger were being mouthed by the assembled gentry.

"Away, ya big fat greasy cow, yer lying on ma fucken' legs — Get yer arse aff ma feet," were but a couple of the expletives! In the meantime, the "Beard", humping the uncouth struggling soldier under his powerful right arm, dumped him into a nearby grease-filmed horse's trough!

It came as no great surprise to Andy and his mates when a blustering bevy of helmeted coppers, hands hovering over their strapped truncheons, appeared from around the corner in Wilson Street and launched a concerted attack on the whole struggling mass of bodies, closely followed by a couple of Black Marias from the precincts of the Sheriff Court Buildings. The self styled "Reverend" Gilbert McGubligan, the well-known Glasgow Evangelist, stationed at the narrow, bottom end of Hutcheson Street, cast a disdainful sidelong glance at the scene of the Sunday outrage and continued quite unperturbed in his energetic rendering of "Onward Christian Soldiers", ably supported by his choir of "Sunday Songsters".

A False Alarm

HOME GUARD detachments were formed. Men who were medically unfit or beyond the conscription age-limit were enlisted from the public utilities such as the post office, railway companies and the gas and electricity authorities. Some units were based on the bigger factory complexes, such as Weirs of Cathcart, St Rollox Works in Springburn, Collins the publishers and others. Basic military training methods to be used in the event of invasion were applied in recognised depots in and around the City.

Drill halls, normally used by the Territorial Army at Taylor Street, the Cameronians Depot at Coplaw Street and the military establishments and reporting centres for the Home Guard men and women engaged in reserved occupations such as gas and water were recruited into numerous supportive organisations like the Local Defence Volunteers, or the Auxiliary Fire Service. A special constabulary was established.

The whole of the appropriate sections of the civilian population were geared into every possible avenue of preparation against enemy invasion, which many thought was imminent.

France, Belgium and Holland had been overrun. Powerful Nazi forces were now ranged along the whole of the European coastline and were highly concentrated in North West France at the English Channel.

The Special Police Force and the Criminal Investigation Department were fully occupied. They were particularly conscious of the increased militancy of the left wing and radical political parties, most of whom were taking up the anti-war cudgels. The Socialist Party of Great Britain, the Labour and Communist Parties organised street and public hall meetings throughout the working class districts of the City. There were reports of clashes — not always verbal — with right-wing groups. The flag waving and drum beating jingoism of the justification for war and the defence of freedom, the Throne and the British Empire was stepped up in the columns of the Establishment newspapers and on the radio network.

The *Daily Worker* was the only national daily which consistently maintained a politically accurate description of the situation by illustrating the futility of the war at this juncture.

A Call to Action

He that is overcautious will accomplish
little.   — *Schiller*

ALAN called for an extraordinary meeting at Bakunin Hall. A
special announcement was to be made. All Anarchists and
known active sympathisers were contacted personally. The
"Beard" controlled admission and showed exceptional
vigilance in his vetting.

If he or any of the members had any reason to suspect that a
"new face" whose political background could not be
authenticated, then the person was either barred, or was advised
that if found to be a police informer, then frankly, he would
suffer dire retribution.

Dougie introduced Alan to the well-attended meeting.

"I need hardly remind you that we should not be lulled into a
state of complacency because some of the Parties that count, and
public opinion, seem to indicate a certain sympathy for our
current programme.

"Of course we cannot concur with the manifestos of these
Parties. They are incorrect. However, that is not to say that we
cannot find common ground with them, or that we should
totally reject any coincidence of opinion, or, in certain
situations, joint action. And what is the common factor that we
must grasp in both hands and exploit to the full? THE ANTI-
WAR MOVEMENT!

"With that in mind, arrangements are under way to organise the
most powerful anti-war demonstration and rally that has ever
been witnessed in the City of Glasgow. Now, as to the air of
secrecy and caution associated with this meeting it gives me the
greatest pleasure possible to inform you that the highlight of the
demonstration will be the attendance of Jim Roxburgh! It is for
this reason that it is not advisable to name a date or venue at this
stage."

There were muted murmurs of dismay and expressions of
surprise and disbelief at the announcement. The "Beard"
interrupted; "Roxburgh's in a Spanish jail, surely? Wasn't he
captured at Jarama while with the Brigade? As far as I knew he
was thrown into a dungeon near Madrid."

81

Alan couldn't resist a smile. "Jim Roxburgh, whose contribution to the international Anarchist movement is second to none, has escaped from the Fascist jail! Underground sympathisers smuggled him to Lisbon. Jim Roxburgh is in London!"

There was prolonged hand clapping and stamping of feet at the news. "For those of you who don't know about the man's background, Roxburgh was in the forefront of the fight against Fascism for two years in Spain. He was wounded in the struggle at Jarama, was taken prisoner, and, I am informed, was subjected to the vilest tortures imaginable at the hands of his Fascist jailers. He lost many comrades in the field of battle. The beacon of freedom has been extinguished in Spain. I consider it to be our duty to re-kindle the flame of world emancipation, delivered to us by Jim Roxburgh."

There was genuine elation at the news about Jim Roxburgh. As the "Beard" remarked, "damned few are able to escape the clutches of Spanish Fascism."

The victory gained by the reactionary forces in Spain had dealt a damaging blow to all progressive forces throughout the world — not least the Anarchists. The escape had been momentous and was hailed as an inspiration to the whole Labour and Trade Union Movement in Britain.

Alan concluded his statement. "Only a few words. I think we are bound to take maximum advantage of the current situation. We should exploit to the full the sympathy that has been generated by the escape of Jim Roxburgh. Jack ("The Beard") will issue you all with a collecting card illustrating a likeness of Jim Roxburgh and headed with an anti-war slogan. I should like to see these cards filled with the maximum of contributions. I know you will consider this to be unorthodox, but, on this occasion, funds are needed. It is our intention to flood this City with notices that Jim Roxburgh is coming to Glasgow!"

Find the Finance

Ah, take the cash and let the Credit go,
Nor heed the rumble of a distant Drum!
— *Omar Khayyam*

PUBS, Clubs, the Trade Councils, even Gospel and Salvation Army outdoor meetings were inundated with collecting cards and cans in the massive, city-wide exercise by the group in the hunt for funds. Cinema queues, factory gate meetings, public baths and street corner political gatherings were besieged. Anarchists and supporters in Trade Union branches called for an allocation from the General Purposes or Branch Political Funds. The slogan employed throughout the campaign was "A United Front against Fascism and War".

And the success was unprecedented.

Andy, as propaganda organiser, controlled the collection by ruthless motivation.

Nevertheless he felt, personally, that he should express some initiative in the matter. At dusk, one night, he removed four clothes pegs from a line and grabbed a newly washed double-bed-size white sheet in the backcourt at Morrin Square. Stuffing the big sheet into the saddle bag of his bike, he overheard the ominous crash of an upward-flung tenement kitchen window. He had been caught in the act!

The big red blotchy face and bust of the irate housewife filled the window space and roared,

"Ya bloody nyaff. Whit the hell are ye dae'in wi ma sheet? Ma man's just comin doon the sterr tae ye, and he'll brek yer bloody back!"

Andy didn't wait to confirm the truth of the threat and beat an undignified retreat into Weaver Street with the unpacked half of the newly laundered sheet flapping and cracking like a sail in the windstream.

The following morning, while cycling to work, he stopped and pinched another big sheet from an unattended clothes basket on the steps of the Steamie in the Gorbals.

Dougie, not to be outdone — but less inclined to over-exertion — merely whipped a double sheet from his old lady's kip! By arrangement, Olga had agreed to stitch all three white sheets together on her old treadle type Singer, thus creating an enormous white banner. This done, the banner was stretched flat on the cleaned floor of Bakunin Hall.

Olga, exposing hitherto concealed artistic talents, produced a remarkable likeness of Jim Roxburgh — in caricature form — with a broad paint brush and a pot of black paint. The date of the rally and a couple of anti-Fascist slogans were prominently displayed in eighteen inch lettering along the length of the massive banner. When the work of art was completed and thoroughly dried, it was neatly folded and packed away for future use. Andy and Dougie had previously planned on how to make the most effective impact with the banner.

Conspiracy

When moral courage feels that it is in the right, there is no personal daring of which it is incapable.   — *Leigh Hunt*

DOUGIE had filled a couple of collection cans with contributions from the railway carters and the trace horse boys. Andy had scrounged a fair amount from his mates at work and on the apprentices committee.

This had been comparatively simple. Andy could confirm that the financial response from the working class had been magnificent.

However, they both agreed that the funds should be topped up by their personal efforts, and, in accordance with current Anarchist thought, this could best be done by utilising a path of direct action.

They discussed a number of ideas. Some of Dougie's suggestions were erratic and immature and would have landed them both in Duke Street Prison. Andy said, "By all means, use the System to our advantage. Consider the risks carefully. Lower the odds on being nabbed. I've no intention of being behind bars. I want to be around on the streets when the demonstration takes place."

A plan of action was finally agreed upon which involved the

84

minimum risk. Initially, it included a pub crawl in order to carry out a survey. The equivalent jargon in the current spate of American gangster movies was known as "casing the joint". Neither of them were confirmed boozers, although lately Douglas had acquired a distinct taste for a jug on the slightest pretext. Visits were made to the proliferation of pubs in the Townhead and adjacent districts. The Tolbooth Bar at Glasgow Cross was given the once-over but was rejected due to its being located too near to the local Central Police Station. They agreed to restrict the bevvy level in each pub to a pint apiece.

The Cot Bar in Castle Street, the College in High Street and the Cross Keys in Rottenrow were scrutinised, but were found to lack the essential requirements. As each pub was investigated the Plan required an adjournment to the cludgie. Andy usually adopted a "look out" position at the bar, while Dougie carried out an inspection of the structure of the lavy.

There were other important considerations: the Plan required that the pub be located in a quiet thoroughfare — particularly where vehicular traffic was concerned. Seemingly insurmountable obstacles cropped up in their fairly widespread survey. Frustration crept in.

At one stage, Andy concluded, "Christ, we can't go on like this for much longer or we will be carted into the Looney Bin as Alkies. I was never that keen on the booze anyway. I'll soon be as bad as the Old Man if I carry on like this for much longer." Dougie, ever mindful of the importance of the Cause — apart from the regular consumption of pints of heavy, responded in the appropriate, political fashion, "Well, stop your bloody moaning. After all, it's all part of the struggle for World Emancipation."

Andy, for a change, could not venture a fitting reply to Dougie's devastating observation!

They agreed that a final effort would be made on a selected Friday night, when the boozer's till was generally filled to capacity with the workers' weekly wage.

If the survey proved unsuccessful, then serious thought would be given to Dougie's insistence on a straightforward hold-up of one of the local banks.

One or two pubs were checked out in St James Road and in Stirling Road. On leaving the Stirling Castle with about half an hour to closing time they wandered, dejectedly, into one of the most frequented howffs in the district — The Grapes Bar in Parson Street.

The Grapes, off the beaten track, provided an ideal catchment hostelry catering for punters from McAslin Street, St Mungo and Stanhope Streets and other densely populated tenements including Parliamentary Road.

Andy, thoroughly depressed, decided to lash out — financially — in this, their final watering-hole, and ordered two halfs and two beers. Swiftly couping the hard stuff with one deft stroke, Dougie went for a much needed pee. He had gone for at least five minutes. A piss didn't take that long surely? Andy decided to follow up. He assumed that Dougie had opted for the luxury of a crap.

As he went towards the door of the "Gents", Dougie appeared with a slightly glazed but unmistakable glint of triumph in his eye. With a barely perceptible wink towards Andy, he swaggered to the bar.

Andy went into the "Gents". Adopting the normal, unconcerned stance common to men the world over, his pee designed inconsequential patterns on the brown stained white enamel of Shanks' urinal while casting furtive glances around the pissery.

"Where the hell is it?" he asked himself. Exaggerating the final shake, he made a last, fruitless examination. "It certainly wasn't here."

Buttoning up, he made a swift entry into one of the two cubicles. The door, which didn't have a snib, reached almost to the ceiling. Removing his shoes, he placed them on the floor so that the toes peered below the lip of the door, indicating that the keich house was occupied. Standing on the bowl, he grasped the greasy cistern and hauled himself upwards. This was when he saw it, in the gloomy ceiling area. It couldn't have been better. A trapdoor, opening into the loft — and held down with a hasp and staple — and no padlock!

Horse Sense

Animals are such agreeable friends; they
ask no questions, pass no criticisms.
— *George Eliot*

DOUGIE had been a capable trace horse lad for some time. He had gained enough experience that would have justified his elevation to the lofty rank of a fully fledged carter. But he preferred the comparative freedom of his present role. Not for him the slow moving, rumbling monotony of a heavily loaded cart trundling up High Street or West Nile Street.

Dougie's Clydesdale horse was immaculate. Brilliantly polished leather work. Burnished brass and bronze metalwork that flashed and flickered like fire in the sunlight. The brightly coloured plumes spraying upwards from the big silver star mounted on the horse's forehead, the well groomed, sleek, brown and white hide with an ornately plaited tail amply displayed Dougie's proud interest in the sturdy animal's welfare and presentation.

Having discarded a tow at the top of High Street, Dougie cantered down Drygate to the John Knox Inn opposite the Great Eastern Hotel. The Inn was the local haunt of the carters from Tennents Brewery in the Ladywell at the Molendinar. Tethering his mount to a street grating, he left the Clydesdale guzzling a half filled canvas bag of oats and joined the inmates of the Inn, where he had some acquaintances, and where he was readily accepted as "one of the boys".

Over a foaming pint, he very soon gleaned the information he needed — the day and approximate time of delivery of barrels of draught beer to The Grapes in Parson Street. He duly imparted the vital information to Andy.

Dougie had done well, Andy thought. He had located the trap door in the pub, and had confirmed the date of the beer delivery. He felt that he was bound to make a personal contribution to the Plan himself, so decided to take the following Tuesday morning off work — the day of the delivery.

Arriving early, Andy criss-crossed Martyr Street and Parson Street repeatedly on his bike, until Tennent's gleaming, spotlessly clean, black and white cart hove into sight as it turned into Parson Street from the long haul up Castle Street. It stopped outside The Grapes at ten o'clock.

The carter dismounted, applied a couple of wheel chocks, and rewarded his sweating nag with a feed bag. Short and stocky, the shirt sleeves were rolled up to expose the bulging biceps. He wore a rough canvas apron that reached the uppers of his boots. Sauntering aimlessly across the pavement, he parked his bulky frame against the pub doors. Seeing the nag munching gratefully at its oats, he produced a short stubby tobacco-stained clay pipe from behind the skip stud of his bunnet, and stabbed the wee stem into his purple lips below the Joe Stalin moustache.

Expertly striking a Swan Vesta on his arse, he ignited the evil smelling contents of the pipe, enveloping his face in wreaths of thick black smoke, while spluttering and coughing like a man in the final stages of consumption.

Andy was sure the carter had set his grizzly face on fire!

He was viewing the scene from a tenement close mouth next to the doctor's surgery across the street. Unscrewing the tyre valve, he deliberately released the air from the rear wheel of his bike.

Walking the machine across the street, towards the pub doors, he turned it upside down a few yards from the carter and went through the motions of repairing the "puncture".

As he removed the chain and wheel, the carter kicked the hell out of the surface-mounted twin steel doors of the beer delivery entry on the pavement, so as to attract the cellar man's attention. The ear splitting clang of the carter's heel plate on the doors frightened the shit out of the contented cart horse. Stomping vigorously with one of its rear legs on the cobbled street surface, it snorted angrily into its feed poke, sending a flurry of brown oats into the air, while casting a reproachful, sidelong glance with its big brown eyes towards its master.

There was a short lived peaceful pause in the proceedings. Suddenly the heavy steel batwing doors of the cellar entry flew upwards and over, striking the pavement with a resounding crash! The belching clay pipe shot clean out of the blustering, gaping gob of the shit-scared carter! The panic stricken horse leapt clear into the air, tossing the feed bag and its contents in the general direction of the gawping carter.

One of the three big beer barrels pitched clear of its wedges, couped off the rear of the platform, and careered drunkenly down Parson Street! The big barrel bounded into the base of a street gas lamp standard, and smashed the glass panes of the lantern at the top of the pole into smithereens, with shards of glass tinkling merrily over the whole disastrous scene.

Across the street, the wee bow-tied sawbones, stethoscope dangling round his scrawny neck and bouncing off his paunchy belly shot out of the surgery entrance to see what the hell had happened, and expecting the worst! He and his patients thought there had been a traffic accident as they streamed into the street.

A big broad beetroot faced and gleaming baldy nut, appeared ominously over the edge of the cellar opening.

"Who in the name of Christ was hammerin' oan ma bloody doors?" he yelled. "Dae youse a' think a'm fucking deef?" He spied the carter spreadeagled on the deck with fright. "Wis it you, ya dosey lookin' cunt, am gon tae brek your fucken neck!" The carter, deserting all responsibility for his horse, beer and carriage, beat a hasty retreat towards the doubtful refuge of the doctor's surgery with Baldy roaring and jumping like a bull in hot pursuit.

"Away ya bowly legged wee bastard," he bawled. "Yer nuthin' but a scaby wee whoremaister!"

Andy, meanwhile, kept his cool and surveyed the sordid scene. He was particularly concerned with the design of the interior of the cellar doors, now fully exposed for his inspection. Exploiting the current commotion to the full, he meandered towards the open doors and noticed that each of them had a simple L-shaped bracket attached to its edge. A long, iron bar, pivoted on a central span in the opening confirmed the method of security.

Hastily inflating his rear tyre, Andy got off his mark. As far as he could see, his presence — and his departure — had been entirely unnoticed.

Unarmed Robbery

Get good counsel before you begin; and
when you have decided, act promptly.
— *Sallust*

ANDY met Dougie on the night following the survey of The Grapes. They discussed their findings and concluded that the Plan was quite conceivable. They agreed that the idea should be shared with Alan and Olga since they would ultimately be involved in the collection and distribution of funds — from whatever source. Anyway, their longer experience in the Movement would reveal any weaknesses in the Plan.

They all met at Alan's place.

On hearing the details, Olga expressed grave doubts. She seemed, to Andy, to be less concerned about the fact that they would be jailed, if caught, than whether the Movement could afford the loss of two activists at such a critical period in the campaign. Dougie had the same impression, on hearing her comments. "Heartless bugger," he thought.

Alan approved wholeheartedly and supported the Plan with his usual political analysis. "I have no hesitation in supporting the venture," he said. "From your description it hardly seems likely that you will have to resort to physical violence. As Anarchists of course, we are not opposed to the use of force. The System, don't forget, will use every available weapon in its well stocked arsenal to maintain its authority. That is the underlying reason for this war. Naturally, if it can possibly be avoided, then we should discourage the use of force against fellow-members of the working class.

"But we are not pacifists, and if force is found to be the means to an end, then it should not be discounted. If we are confirmed in our beliefs, as Anarchists, then we must consider the violent overthrow of the State to be completely justified.

"Therefore I approve of the Plan. I would however, attach one very important condition. If, under any circumstances, an activist is apprehended in his or her work, any association with the Anarchist Federation will be emphatically denied. In other words, you must both consider yourselves as being completely isolated while carrying out the Plan. This applies to all of us, at all times. The correctness of this principle will, I am sure, be apparent to you, in time."

Saturday night was chosen for reasons that were all too obvious. The Grapes, as usual, was packed to the gunnels with beer and ale swilling customers. They were clustered, four deep, around the entire length of the horseshoe-shaped bar. The pitch of the men's voices were raised in direct proportion to the number of gallons consumed.

Arguments raged over the widest range of subjects imaginable. In the far corner, Joe Louis and Benny Lynch discarded their jackets. The bunnets were slung into the spit and sawdust polished floor and they squared up to each other with totally ineffectual fists. As they advanced, aggressively, towards each other, they dared all and sundry to step in and prevent the oncoming slaughter.

There were no takers among the customers.

Baldy, the cellar man, grabbed them both by the scruff of the neck and the arse of the baggy trousers and propelled them rapidly through the double doors into the street, followed by the flying jackets.

Spilled beer swirled and eddied on the polished bar surface and dripped into the sawdust-filled trough below the bashed brass foot rail.

Hitler, Franco and that "fat tally bastard", Mussolini, were being lambasted without mercy. King William of Orange and His Holiness, the Pope, were being indiscriminately fucked all over the place. Faintly concealed and badly fumbled Orange and Masonic handshakes were being exchanged, accompanied by knowing winks — though damned few of them had ever entered a church, never mind the portals of a Masonic temple. Neville Chamberlain was being vigorously vilified and crude suggestions being made as to where he should insert his umbrella. It was even suggested that once inserted, it should be opened and withdrawn!

Opinions on Churchill were wide and varied. Leon Trotsky, Stalin — and Jim Roxburgh — were being eulogised, in the main.

Andy, on entering the pub, was unaccompanied, and selected an unobtrusive perch on the end of a grimy bench in one of the inshots below a lead-latticed window advertising India Pale Ale. The atmosphere was polluted with writhing tobacco smoke from a hundred Woodbine fags and a bevy of belching clay pipes.

Dougie came in and chose to support a corner of the bar, well distanced from Andy. He had just enough for two pints, Andy having insisted on retaining the balance of his cash. Andy knew that Dougie was liable to over-imbibe and become involved in a political argument. The job in hand required two sober minds.

The beer-sodden cash, mainly coinage, rapidly filled the two wooden, six-bowled money drawers, located at each end of the well-stocked mirrored gantry. Being a Saturday night, there was a fairly consistent slap of the spring clip on an ever-thickening bundle of ten bob and one pound notes.

Baldy operated the drawer nearest the front door while his mate controlled the other. At about eight o'clock, Barney Robertson, the proprietor, with subtle movements developed over the years, removed the overflowing bowls from their recesses and skilfully emptied them into a deep, black enamelled steel box containing a removable tray for the notes. The box seemed to be screwed to the floor behind a wee door under the end of the gantry.

Dougie thought it would probably be the compartment containing the gas and electric meters. It needed a sharp, sober — and interested — eye to watch Barney adroitly extracting the bowls and notes and momentarily half disappear into the wee cupboard as though searching for spirits.

Around ten minutes before closing time, Andy vacated his pew and headed for a pee.

Dougie similarly inclined, followed him into the "Gents". The joint was jumping, and their separate departures were unobserved.

Fortunately, there were two adjacent and unoccupied urinals. Nonchalantly scrutinising the intricacies of the spluttering Shanks overhead cistern — and their respective pissers — Andy controlled his peeing pace while Dougie took up residence in the nearby cubicle. The half-stewed old bugger using the third urinal was perched precariously on the inner edge of the marble platform with his nut balanced against the tiled wall and his hands dug deep into his trouser pockets. He was taking too bloody long to finish off and Andy wondered whether he had dozed off. He seemed oblivious to everything, but Andy bade his time.

Finally, pissed off, the man headed for the door, still shaking his wrinkled blue-veined fella in his hands as he made his faltering exit. As soon as the man had left the cludgie, Andy darted in beside Dougie. It occurred to him that Barney the proprietor wouldn't have reacted too well to such an arrangement in his lavy! Dougie being the tallest, was just able to reach up and flick the hasp from the staple on the trapdoor. He produced a short crowbar which he strapped to the calf of his leg. He poked the trapdoor gently. It was loose, and lightly hinged. Just then, they heard Baldy bawling "Time!" in the pub as another three men staggered into the piss-house. Time was becoming a vital factor.

At any moment there would be a last-minute invasion by the drunken horde to relieve themselves. Already, there was someone thumping hell out of their cubicle door — no room at the urinal! Andy growled his presence, while the man grumbled something about it "it being a fine bloody time to pick for having a shite!" There was now no time to dally. Baldy would soon be in to clear out the stragglers.

Andy stood upright, feet apart on the bowl with his back against the wall. Dougie adopted a similar position opposite Andy whose hands were cupped and clasped to take Dougie's big foot. Dougie reached upwards with the crowbar. In the high pitched cacophony of drunken men's voices nobody seemed to hear the trapdoor being levered upwards and landing with a dull thud inside the loft. He tossed the crowbar into the opening. It was now or never.

Dougie placed his right foot firmly in the clasp, and, momentarily grasping Andy's shoulders, leapt straight through the open ceiling. Andy was sure he had burst a gut as he used every ounce of his strength in Dougie's elevation. Dougie had disappeared from view, and the trapdoor swung gently into its original position.

Andy opened the cubicle door to a chorus of curses and abuse, left the lavy, and met Baldy heading for the Cludgie Clearance!

Dougie's troubles had just started. Leaping into the pitch black loft had taken a terrible toll on his elbows, while his snout had collided with a discarded beer crate. He settled on the

93

upturned crate and nursed his injuries, while lighting up a Woodbine. He would smoke a few before his stint was over. A swift scurrying of little feet indicated that he would not be alone in his vigil! His thoughts raced back to a previous confrontation with the rats as schoolboys in the Townhead pumping station. His mate, Andy, still bore the scars!

When Andy left the pub he headed for Gizzie's ice cream shop in Parliamentary Road for a hot plate of mushy peas, liberally drowned in vinegar. As he sat in one of the booths he felt a genuine concern for Dougie.

The Plan involved a time lapse and this fact appeared to be the most frustrating feature of the whole idea. He thought for a moment that he should go back to The Grapes.

"What purpose would that serve?" he asked himself. He rejected the thought immediately. Why the hell did he even think of it? A definite lack of control over himself, that was why!

He thought of the scene in the pub. The environment in The Grapes was typical of all the pubs and clubs in the Townhead, and for that matter of all the other pubs in the city, other cities, other countries! Why did the men in the pub seem so unconcerned about the need for change?

Why did their horizons seem to be restricted to half-drunk, meaningless conversation, in a smoke-ridden, dimly-lit pub on a Saturday night? He couldn't, for a moment, accept that the State, in its manipulations, could be so effective. Could the men not see the *real* situation as he did, as all the other activists saw it? If all the men, in all the pubs, in all of the cities, and in all nations, could unite — even for a short period — in a concerted attack on the State administration, then no force in the world could repel their overwhelming strength. Perhaps they needed a British Lenin?

Does a man become immune to the harsh inequalities in society as he grows older?

Does he lose faith in his fellow men?

The facilities and organisations were readily available. Why did they not join the Communist Party?

Why would they not do as he and Dougie had done and take up the cudgels of Anarchism and smash the whole corrupt bloody citadel to smithereens? He was more than ever convinced of the need for the violent destruction of the State apparatus. Surely all working men — and the unemployed — would, within themselves, agree that there was need for an upheaval? Certainly the Labour Party and the I.L.P. could boast a mass following. But they spoke of "seizure", "reformism" and "Parliamentary change".

The doctor doesn't prescribe aspirin for cancer! The State cancer would have to be ruthlessly exorcised — and the Anarchists would wield the scalpel!

The café was beginning to fill up with cinemagoers from the local Casino and Carlton picture houses. There was still about an hour and a half to wait before the action. He wandered towards the Night Star in Alexandra Parade and bought two fish suppers, double wrapped in an extra sheet of the *Sunday Post*, and went to see Alan.

There was no light in the kitchen window as he looked up from the street. Alan and his old lady were still out somewhere, or they were in bed. Either way, he didn't relish the thought of devouring two fish suppers after Gizzie's green peas. He struck the brass door knocker gently, and noticed in the glimmer of the spluttering stairhead light, that the knocker was shaped in the form of a wee Buddha.

Alan eventually answered the foor, clad in his shorts and semit. The smell of the fresh fish suppers clinched the muttered welcome. He lit the oven and popped the grub inside on a dinner plate for a quick re-heat.

Over a mug of tea, while intermittently wiping his greasy fingers in his oxter, Andy brought Alan up-to-date on the pub robbery. Although fairly confident of its success he hoped inwardly that Alan might offer to accompany him back to The Grapes. He must have betrayed his thoughts.

"Andy, I daresay you wouldn't object to my coming to The Grapes with you, but, as I have said before you must handle the situation yourselves. You and Dougie have worked hard at the project. If it proves successful, you will have the satisfaction of knowing that you didn't call for assistance.

"Anyway, I can assure you that my role in the Movement is recorded in the police files, and frankly, I can accept that. It is to be expected. It was no accident, by the way, when the copper flopped in the door of Bakunin Hall on the night of your first visit.

"Never underestimate their prowess in the gathering of intelligence. The State is far more interested in the movements of a political or trade union activist than in the actions of the petty criminal. And that is why I cannot be associated with you tonight. If you and Dougie are nabbed, then the crime will be seen as breaking and entering, and nothing more, as I don't suppose you will be on their register as yet.

"If I was found to be even remotely connected, the effect would be devastating. They would make a political feast of the incident and probably smash the nucleus of the Federation in Glasgow. As a matter of fact, Andy, you should not have come to see me at all tonight!"

Andy was taken aback, momentarily. But Alan's message had got through and he decided to make no reply to his constructive criticism. He realised that he had made a bad, political blunder.

At eleven forty-five, he left Alan, walked along Stirling Road and, on reaching Barony Street, the clock tower on the Royal Infirmary showed ten minutes to midnight. He stood just inside a close next to Teachers Pub.

In the pitch blackness of the loft at The Grapes, Dougie had been using his shoes as an ashtray for his Woodbines. He had smoked a packet of ten. He withdrew the spent fag ends and popped them into his trousers pocket, lifted the crowbar, opened the trapdoor, lowered himself on to the lip of the lavatory pan, lined up the hasp and fitted it over the staple. There wasn't much he could have done about the fag fumes drifting around inside the loft.

The pub was as quiet as a graveyard. He thoroughly enjoyed a long-drawn-out, much needed pee. On entering the bar, the stink of stale beer and the blanket of foul smelling tobacco smoke caught his breath and nearly choked him. Crouching, he ducked under the polished bar flap and went directly to the gas meter cupboard.

Using the tapered chisel of the crowbar, he soon had the cash box prised from the floor. He noticed that this particular section of the gantry was illuminated by a dangling low wattage light bulb. He realised this was for the benefit of the beat cop, and, of course, the publican.

He was busily fixing the crowbar to his leg strap when the pub door was suddenly shaken violently. In the quietness of the pub, Dougie felt sure that the door was being battered off its hinges. He began to wonder if some bugger might have had the cheek and audacity to contemplate robbing the premises by a frontal assault on the main door!

Some folk, he thought, simply had no sense of decency and decorum at all! He made a dive for the cork matting covering the cellar door entry and then realised that the noisy culprit was the patrolling beat cop making an exaggerated check on the pub security.

Dropping flat on his belly, the deep smoky gloom was suddenly swathed by a bright dazzling beam of light from the cop's torch. "Some torch," he thought. The cone of light danced ponderously from one end of the bar to the other.

Fortunately, he had re-closed the gas meter door — and the cash box was below the level of the bar. The cop moved on.

Then Dougie was confronted with his first major obstacle. On lifting the cork matting he found the cellar door had been secured to the floor by a massive glinting galvanised padlock that would have been more beneficially employed on the main gates at Barlinnie Jail!

It was at least three inches square and as thick as his thumb! He felt the first dull pangs of uncertainty and panic in his guts. Quite apart from the cash, he realised that he was trapped on the premises.

A quick glance at the brown face of the pub clock didn't help matters. Andy would be hovering around outside. It was five minutes to midnight! He should have been in the cellar by this time. Would the beat cop still be hanging around? It would need a stick of dynamite or a sledge hammer to move the monstrosity. The wee crowbar would never move it in a month of Sundays!

He aimed a vicious kick at the offending obstacle, and was rewarded with a badly stubbed set of toes on his right foot. Addressing the padlock in the popular Glasgow idiom as being "a fuck pig's bastard!" his attention was diverted to the hinged section of the cellar door.

It was now three minutes to twelve.

It had been agreed that Andy should get off his mark at midnight since it would have attracted the police attention to have loitered at the pub door, at such a late hour. And Dougie knew that Andy would "shoot the crow" if he didn't move his arse a bit rapidly!

He blootered the crowbar into the crevice at one of the hinges, angled the tool to about forty degrees, jumped on it with both feet and wrenched the end of the door away from the floor.

This had taken a couple of minutes. Andy would be wondering what the hell was happening as the crash of splintering timber must have been heard by everyone within earshot.

It was midnight.

He grabbed the cash box and leapt down the short flight of steps into the cellar.

Andy strolled along Parson Street towards the steel plates at The Grapes, stopped to light a cigarette and gently tapped the doors with his heel. He had heard the commotion from inside the pub.

The beat cop, luckily, had just turned into McAslin Street from Martyr Street and had just missed the racket by seconds. On hearing the taps on the steel doors, Andy swivelled the securing bar, opened one flap of the opening — which he supported — while the box was thrown up on to the pavement. Dougie shot up through the opening like a bat out of Hell, then both of them replaced the door flap.

They knew every close, alleyway, dyke and back court in the district, so were able to wend their way, without interference or detection, to the Rottenrow.

Reaching the comparative safety of Cathedral Court, they carted the box up the five storey tenement to the almost disused wash-house on the flat roof.

It struck Dougie as ironic that the money box was totally insecure after experiencing the pulse-racing confrontation with the bloody big padlock.

The box contained three hundred and ten pounds!

A well-directed throw from the top balcony of the tenement block, and the black box splashed into the steel tank reservoir of the pumping station.

Organs of the State

It is the old practice of despots to use a
part of the people to keep the rest in
order.   — *Jefferson*

CHIEF CONSTABLE Jack Sillars convened a special
conference in the Central Division Briefing Room at Turnbull
Street, off Saltmarket. Senior Officers of the Serious Crime
Squad led by Chief Superintendent Alex Galloway were
present; Sillars had also called on the services of the leading
officers of the Police Transport Section with special interest in
the railway networks controlled by the L.N.E.R. and the
L.M.S. The Chief Constable bore a striking resemblance to "Il
Duce", Benito Mussolini — a big broad stubby thrusting chin,
topped by a hard-lipped gub like a skinny letter box opening,
and a broad purple snout. He was aware of the physical
similarity and acted the part accordingly when the opportunity
cropped up.

When lecturing his minions, from his elevated podium, he
spoke loudly and shouted as though he was addressing a Fascist
rally in Rome. And it was effective.

Lighting up a wee fat cigar, and jabbing it into his kisser, he
started sounding off, with the stubby cigar oscillating like the
vane of a windmill.

"The City Police Committee have received an application for
permission to organise a demonstration and march along the
accepted Route from Blythswood Square to the South End of
North Frederick Street at George Square. It was submitted by
the Glasgow City Committee of the Labour Party. They clearly
defined the purpose of the demonstration as being primarily
concerned with their demand for a reduced working week in
industry without loss of earnings. The Labour Party also
confirmed that the march would include representatives of the
Glasgow Trades Council and the various Trades Unions
affiliated to the Council.

"The Police Committee recently approved of demonstrations
and rallies by the Orange Lodges and the Order of Hibernians,
with final assemblies at the Glasgow Green and at Queens Park.
Because of this, it was considered inadvisable to show any

discrimination towards the political parties, especially in view of the current strong feelings being expressed by the Labour Party and the I.L.P. But I asked the Committee to adjourn their final decision — something rankled in my mind — and from what I can now reveal, you will agree that my recommendation was correct. "

Sillars was in his element!

The cigar butt had been ruthlessly pounded into the ash tray. The forefinger was jabbing the audience like a short sharp spear. The fist was clenched and thrown outwards. The arms were flailing!

" Until last week there seemed to be no reason to suspect that the Rally would be other than the description contained in the application. I need hardly remind you that our intelligence network is second to none, particularly from our informers in certain political parties.

"Well, gentlemen, I have been advised by a very reliable source of information that the apparently run-of-the-mill Rally is likely to develop into a bloody tidal wave with the possibility of mob violence being generated by certain foreign-inspired political elements. I don't think I should have to enter into detail on that score.

" It is unfortunate that vestiges of the political scum that left this country — and Glasgow — managed to survive and have come back here with even more inflated ideas about changing the system and other preposterous suggestions. The Met have confirmed this and have detailed lists of the names and activities of the bastards.

"What concerns me is the fact that they are spreading their tentacles into all of the major industrial centres in this country — including Glasgow. And this is where we should have the benefit of the wide experiences of Chief Super. Galloway. Alex," he growled, "your comments, if you please."

"Thank you, Sir. Most of you know my background well enough. The Chief mentioned my experience in the political arena, and I suppose it was inevitable that I would pick up a few tit-bits while in charge of the Squad in London, particularly in Ridley Road and the Brick Lane.

"One thing has become clear to me since coming back to Glasgow, and that is that you lads haven't had to contend with an Oswals Mosley! Now he is some man! He is like a political magnet that could attract Reds, Anarchists and Jews from every nook and cranny from the predominantly working-class, slum areas of London.

"The political scene in London is fairly clear cut, and easily defined. Two contending factions. On the one hand, black uniforms fronting a mob of supporters with their right arms outstretched and demanding a Clean, White Jew-free Britain. On the other hand, Communists, Jews and Trotskyites — with left-wing elements of the Labour Party and the I.L.P. flourishing the Red clenched fist, and all of them — men, women and even children — calling for the annihilation of the Fascists and demanding an end to this war! Lads, I hope you will never have to witness such fanatical determination in Glasgow. To hear thousands of raised voices in a combined, tremendous roar of '*They shall not pass*', is an experience which, to my mind, is quite unforgettable.

"As to Glasgow. On the Chief's instructions, a select squad of my men have spent the last few weeks on infiltration posing as interested listeners — and sometimes as members — at indoor and public street meetings, and gathering important names and information. My squad have lockers full of well worn bunnets and raincoats — and they use them — I can assure you! At this moment I have suitably attired officers standing at the pub bars in the city, absorbing information which I intend to use in the very near future.

"Occasionally, you may find a 'bent' copper in the ranks, but you will rarely, if ever, find one who is politically 'bent'. And, of course, the lesson here is obvious. The State guarantees a well-fed, well-paid and satisfied Force as its first line of defence in the maintenance of law and order. That's why the Force is hardly likely to bite the hand that feeds it!

"Now, gents, this meeting was called to acquaint you all with certain important facts. One of my informants, a member of one of the larger political Parties, made a personal arrangement to meet me and I think you should be made aware of the substance of the conversation I had with him. All of the orthodox Parties are convinced that the forthcoming Rally has been initiated by one or other of the mainstream organisations. I felt that the information divulged to me by the informant should be shared

101

with our Chief Constable. The Chief and I subsequently agreed on the presentation of these facts. We are now in a position to confirm that one of the shrewdest manoeuvres in Glasgow's political history is about to be perpetrated on the people of this city! Certain well known agitators and orators will lead the march and address the Rally.

"This is acceptable, and, to date, we can credit ourselves as having been well-equipped to control the emotional outbursts and incitement to riot. However, gents, on this occasion we are faced with a potentially more dangerous situation than any that we have previously handled. I can categorically confirm that the main spokesman and propagandist at the conclusion of the March will be Roxburgh of the Anarchist Federation! Having proved this, you can take it from me that the planning and organisation of this massive demonstration has been motivated not by the Labour Party — but by the Anarchists!

"Men, if this revolutionary bastard and his cronies have established the leadership of this demonstration, then more than half of the working class in Glasgow will be on the streets to support him. They are convinced that Roxburgh is the British Joe Stalin!"

The Chief thanked Galloway, and addressed Arnison of the Police Transport Section. "Tom, we know absolutely everything about this man Roxburgh. He has been in Spain for some time now and we regret that he has returned. The Metropolitan Police Force thought they had seen the last of him. It was not to be. The man has gained an international reputation. He utterly rejects the theories of 'seizure' and 'change' and 'reformism' etc., with which terms we have become acquainted. This man advocates the destruction, the complete overthrow of the whole State apparatus!

"Christ Almighty! that's what he tried to do in Spain. And he is coming to Glasgow! We will know shortly when he is expected to arrive. I will advise your Department when I know from London. The Met. are already on the job. Tom, I want you to maintain the normal level of uniformed presence at the Central Station on his arrival. He will be accommodated by Glasgow members of their Federation or by sympathisers. Somehow, I cannot imagine Roxburgh taking up residence at the Central or Grosvenor Hotels.

"Now, Superintendent Galloway has arranged for one or two of his men to infiltrate the reception committee. Alex will go into greater detail with you later. One of Alex's men, he tells me, will actually be a fellow passenger in Roxburgh's coach. Don't, for a moment, underestimate the importance of this assignment. This man and his associates are extremely dangerous characters. There is nothing more to be said, gentlemen, except that I want to know Roxburgh's contacts in Glasgow. And I want the information on my desk within an hour of his arrival!"

A Social Gathering

War is the greatest plague that can afflict humanity; it destroys religion, it destroys states, it destroys families. Any scourge is preferable to it.
— *Martin Luther*

A WELL-DRESSED young man booked the Conference Room and Buffet facilities at the Belford Hotel in Sauchiehall Street. The arrangement was for a one-night-stand. Financial business was concluded and the booking confirmed. Extra payment was made to ensure that a competent person would be posted, permanently at the door of the suite. His duty would be to verify that the participants would be in possession of a form of identification which the young man duly described to the manager. He complied, willingly.

Appointments of this nature, with payment on the nail, were not a regular feature of the hotel's business during the early months of the war. He remarked to the cashier, "the military authorities seem to be monopolising everything in the city with their NAAFI Institute in Buchanan Street, their commandeering of the Grand at Charing Cross, and I hear that they have designs on the Grosvenor. Remind the staff to lay on a good service. If we do well enough we may get repeat bookings."

The function had been paid for and authorised by the "Taylor Street Drill Hall Home Guard Social Committee". There would be no dancing! No festivities! No waitress service had been requested. The only conditions were that the buffet facilities should be liberally laced with an adequate supply from the wine cellar — and complete privacy.

The Chief Constable looked forward to the session at the Belford. " Surely to Christ there will be drink in a hotel? " It was known that he was opposed to strong drink at police briefings and the like since it was not conducive to discipline and good order.

It was also known that he packed a flask in the hippie! The social committee, ten strong, were duly identified, admitted to the suite, and were shown to their seats — with not a uniform in sight.

Colonel Eglinton-Harris, the Officer Commanding the Highland Light Infantry at Maryhill Barracks, invited the Chief Constable to occupy a seat on his right.

The Colonel was flanked, on his left, by his Adjutant, Major Hicks.

Hicks, a short arsed backle, wore a kilt and sported skinny wee legs like a deformed speug!

Inspector Anderson of the City Special Constabulary was ranged alongside the Chief Constable. He had retired from the Regular Force, but had been recalled to take charge of the Specials in the war emergency. He had an exemplary track record as a fanatical opponent of trades unionism; picket line and strike busting; and general harassment of the Labour Movement. He was perhaps best known for his involvement in having Gallacher, Shinwell and others dumped into Duke Street Jail as a younger man. The working class in Glasgow knew him as a bloody neo-Fascist — which was why he was *really* recalled!

Eglinton-Harris, a product of the line of Eglintons who owned and controlled vast tracts of agricultural land and coal mines in Ayrshire and Wigtownshire from time immemorial, was intensely proud of his land-owning, aristocratic origins. He had decided, early in his life, that his destiny lay in the continuation of his heritage of distinction — class distinction!

Physically and mentally capable in all respects, he chose the military machine as his vehicle for retaining some vestige of the old traditions; if not at home — then in the Colonies. The yokels

104

of the Scottish peasantry and the agitating Red scum in his coal-fields had somewhat eroded the former glories and splendour of near slavery and serfdom on his stamping ground. He often thought (and kept his beliefs to himself) that capitalism — the home grown variety — was proving a little disappointing. Inwardly, he envied the Krupps and the Thyssens in Europe. Their possessions were well protected. In fact they were developing — and at some rate!

"Why the Hell could we not cultivate the Hitlers and Francos in Britain?" These yellow-bellied politicians in Whitehall had let the side down badly!

He had attended Glasgow University. From there it was Eton — then Sandhurst.

The tea monopolies were expressing some concern about the sporadic uprisings in the plantations of India, and this was reflected in the powerful lobby in the Commons and Lords. The War Office responded in the time-honoured fashion with gunboat military contingents being dispatched post-haste. At that particular time there was no open military conflict on the international scene with which the War Office might be otherwise engaged.

The big armaments manufacturers, however, were baying for blood — and profit! They were screaming for a legitimate outlet for their products. This, coupled with the demands of the tea barons for immediate intervention forced the War Office into justifying its role in society.

Eglinton-Harris thought that if these damned Socialists ever gained control of the reins of power, the whole warmongering leadership might become unemployed! And who could imagine an Admiral or a General signing on at the Broo!

The firm control and extension of the frontiers of the British Colonial Empire presented an ideal opportunity for the likes of Colonel Eglinton-Harris to demonstrate their God-sent prowess at "administration"!

The French Imperialists were occupied in Africa and the Far East. So were the Italians and Portuguese. Indeed, if we didn't enter into the fray bloody quick, we could lose out to the Japanese militarists, not to mention the U.S.A.

The canon-fodder was readily available from the ranks of the unemployed, and, as Eglinton-Harris could verify, from experience, what better choice than the Scottish Regiments to take the lead with the skirl of the pipes and the swinging of the kilt with the flashing of the bayonet. . . .

The Ladies from Hell!

Poverty and starvation was rampant in Rawalpindi. Rebellions were becoming commonplace in the Punjab and in Karachi.

In Bombay, the only natives who waxed fat were the Colonialist-backed racketeers and the bloated rat population at the Docks. The chances of an average Indian native reaching the age of thirty-five were remote.

Hundreds of thousands of Sikhs, Hindus and Moslems, protesting against the pittance of a livelihood allocated by the rich tea merchants were forced, finally, into massive revolt. Religious differences were temporarily cast aside in the common struggle.

The Indian Princes and Government House appealed to the starving people's sense of proportion and reason! But an empty belly makes a poor listener!

Gandhi called for non-violent demonstration and pacifism. British barracks and military outposts were raided by sabre and club wielding young Indians. Gradually, an arsenal of weapons and ammunition was accumulated. Centres of revolution were established in the Khyber Pass and in the border areas of Afghanistan.

Eglinton-Harris was, by now, fully acclimatised, and, flushed with Sandhurst jingoism, went out from Delhi to suppress a particularly well-armed army of insurgents at the Khyber Pass. The Force was formed from the ranks of the Highland Light Infantry and the Queen's Own Cameron Highlanders.

Andy's Father was one of the unsung heroes with the latter! The demands of the rebels (the British Government described them as terrorists!) were not excessive.

"Bread and Freedom" was the dominant slogan which was supported by the countless multitudes of suppressed Indians throughout the sub-continent.

Entrenched in the arid, rock strewn hillsides and ravines of the Pass, the rebels posed a seemingly impregnable series of fortresses.

Eglinton-Harris recognised this and called up the artillery.

The slopes were mercilessly bombarded for twelve hours without intermission. The Indians, well enough experienced with the man-to-man tactics of struggle, had never been involved in warfare of such tremendous ferocity and destruction. He then sent in the infantry which eventually exterminated the demoralised insurgents with rifle and bayonet, though numbers escaped into the surrounding mountains to reform and continue the struggle.

Five hundred and twenty-six prisoners were taken in the single campaign and transported to the Ravi Concentration Camp at Rawalpindi. The charges levelled against all of the prisoners — by the Military Governor — was "insurrection, without just cause, against the British Colonial Administration of India".

Eglinton-Harris, mindful of the long established principles of British Justice, called upon the services of half-a-dozen high ranking Indian Administrators (usually referred to as puppets) and included them in the Court Defence and Prosecution Staff.

Orders from London had demanded that an example be shown to the rest of the recalcitrant population. Hundreds of local shanty dwellers were rounded up and forcibly marched into the concentration camp where, interspersed with a number of Indian newspaper reporters and photographers, they were to witness the application of democratic justice — Colonial style.

All of the prisoners were found guilty as charged, and shot to death by firing squads in one of the bloodiest massacres ever perpetrated on the long suffering Indian people!

The British-controlled Indian Press reacted as expected, the editorials advising a lowering of tensions, and while condoning the Gandhi-like demonstrations, denounced the terrorist element who were, of course, in the minority. The Vatican condemned the incident unreservedly. *Pravda* called for all religious, tribal and political differences to be buried and for a massive, India-wide, retaliation against the British Imperialist presence by a United Front of the Indian people.

The London *Graphic* stated, "It must be said that by the well-timed application of this most regrettable — but necessary — stroke of authority, our presence in the Colony will have been seen by the mass of the predominantly peaceful Indian peoples as being essential to their continued well being. There are problems, but the British and Indian peoples cannot accuse Mahatma Gandhi. The grisly affair at Rawalpindi was initiated by the insidious Marxist elements intent on the revolutionary overthrow of our presence in Mother India."

Eglinton-Harris was suitably lauded on his homecoming. Bestowed with appropriate military decorations, the "Scourge of Indian Terrorism" was allocated a lucrative desk in the Colonial Office. "Damned fine young chap, Eglinton-Harris. Whipped the bloody rabble into line with one fell stroke. A few more of his calibre are needed for the British backbone. Now, when I was a newly-commissioned young buck in South Africa. Africa...," said the decrepit metal-laden General Arbuthnott from his polished leather perch in the House of Lords.

When all of the invited "Social Committee" members had been vetted and admitted into the Suite at the Belford, the door was locked and the bouncer instructed to retain his post with the promise of a lucrative tip.

Having taken maximum advantage of the buffet offerings, Eglinton-Harris called the guests to order, all of whom were liberally loaded with liquor. He introduced each to the other with a short description of their background histories.

"You are all senior Officers in your respective Agencies, and you must be aware, by now, that the conference has been convened for a very special purpose. I don't intend to monopolise the discussion, and will restrict myself to a short detail of the reason for being here. The Anarchists are planning a massive demonstration and rally in the city.

"The Chief Constable has reason to believe that the situation might become uncontrollable. If this is the case, then we must all become involved, using all the forces available to us. If it is proved that the position is as potentially dangerous as he describes, it cannot be left to the regular Police Force to handle it. I have briefed Major Hicks, and would ask him to open the discussion."

Hicks, his bandy-legged kilted frame perched on a chair that was much too high for him, had not been looking forward to this at all. His wee highly polished silver buckled brogues barely reached the floor, so that his skinny wee shanks were left swinging like a pair of pendulums.

Hicks had distinguished himself in the latter period of the Great War and had subsequently joined the forces of intervention ranged against the revolutionary movement in Russia. He had long since attributed his failure in the promotion stakes to the complete routing of, and near extermination of the interventionists by the young, struggling republic, now well consolidated in the Soviet Government.

Although a soldier by profession, Hicks fancied himself as a well-read political animal. He had recognised the danger inherent in the Peace Treaty that was concluded at Brest-Litovsk between Russia and Germany.

After Lenin's proclamation, on the establishment of Bolshevik rule in Petrograd, Hicks, a youthful lecturer in the Army's Current Affairs Bureau, applied his political prowess to his avowed mission to throttle the Russian Revolution at its inception. Appointed as head of the "Russian Department" at the Aldershot School of Current Affairs, he entered the fray with vigorous and biased discourses. His lectures assumed a fairly consistent trend and were always directed against the menace of Russian Bolshevism. So he addressed his classes:

"The Russian Government is a rabble who were fortunately in a position to exploit the war taking place with Germany. They have virtually no control over the mass of Russian peasantry in that vast country, their power being mainly centred in the Moscow and Petrograd regions. The most influential forces in Russia are not the Bolsheviks but the counter-revolutionary armies which include the cream of the Tsarist Officer Corps and the cadets of the aristocracy. These men incidentally, were as well-trained as our own and their aims are similar.

"Large, well organised armies of men are located in Siberia and northern Russia, all of them controlled by Admiral Kolchak. The same applies in the Baltic States of Latvia, Estonia and Lithuania where the Freedom Movement is being led by General Yudenich.

"All this, coupled with the serious divisions of opinion within the government itself, will guarantee the defeat of Bolshevism. Detachments have already been dispatched to Murmansk and the Baltic countries.

"I have decided that you have been well enough informed during these series of lectures and as well trained officers, you have been specially selected to lead a particularly important expedition. It will be our task to assist in the White Guard campaign in the South Russian front. You may agree that the sub-tropical climate of the Crimea has much to commend it over the wastelands of Siberia!

"The Admiralty are presently preparing a flotilla at Portsmouth and Southampton and the destination will be the Black Sea and the Crimea. A blockade of sea-links with Russia has been set up. All sea and land routes to Russia have been severed. The revolution and its aftermath has ravaged Russia. It has been economically isolated. I want you all to consider this expedition as a Crusade — a Crusade for the extermination of the hordes of athiestic Bolshevism. Some problems have cropped up at the Docks where Bolshie sympathisers are refusing to load our equipment, but our own men have smashed their bloody picket lines. In fact, the Commie organisers are already inside, licking their wounds!"

The Intervention

It is impossible to predict the time and progress of revolution. It is governed by its own more or less mysterious laws. But when it comes, it moves irresistibly!
— *Lenin, 1918*

MAJOR HICKS dispatched his second-in-command to Glasgow and other Scottish centres for the recruitment of the rank-and-file forces of the expedition to South Russia. He found bloody few volunteers, and the Force consisted of Regulars.

The overthrow of the Tsarist Regime and of the reactionary Provisional Government in Petrograd by the Bolsheviks led by Molotov and Stalin (who had returned from exile in Siberia) had a profound effect on the minds of the international working class. The dockers refused to handle material destined for Russia, in ports throughout Europe. Units of the German Navy mutinied. The Spartacists in Germany created havoc.

When Lenin arrived from Switzerland, he assumed personal direction of the uprising in the capital, at the Smolny Institute.

The ministries, railway stations and banks were seized. The Government leader, Kerensky, dressed as a woman, fled from the scene and disappeared into the horizon of history! Lenin declared the establishment of power, and, in his momentous address to the Red Guards, proclaimed, "We will now proceed to construct a Socialist System of Society."

Troops on both sides were openly collaborating on the Russian German Front in Europe. The British Army, mainly conscript, were laying down their arms in the French and Belgian trenches.

"Enough of this senseless slaughter" was the order of the day.

Hicks correctly calculated that the conscripted scum would be totally unreliable in his venture, whereas the tried and tested Regulars, whose minds had been cleverly conditioned to the menace of Bolshevism, could be ordered into line. "After all," Hicks remarked, "that was their job, they had volunteered their services as professional killers!"

Hicks and the chosen Freedom Fighters embarked from Southampton on the destroyer "Fearless". Docking at Marseilles, their numbers were swelled by a horde of mercenaries, embittered French jailbirds, deserters from the Legion and remnants of the White Revolutionaries and bourgeois elements who sincerely believed that the old autocratic order in Russia could be restored!

The counter-revolution in South Russia was led by the Fascist Pole, Pilsudski, and by General Wrangel who had collected the fragments of the defeated Denikin Army. These two gents would not reconcile themselves to the proven impregnability of Soviet Power. They thought they would succeed where the Kolchaks and others had been ignominiously smashed by the well-steeled young Red Army. The expedition was supported by the Governments of France, Great Britain and Germany.

At this time, a number of Bolshevik leaders had been captured on the orders of Wrangel, and with no semblance of a trial were publicly hanged as terrorists in the oilfields of Baku. It was intended that this action would subdue the ferment of

111

revolutionary feeling in the area. It had precisely the opposite effect! They badly underestimated the resolute strength of the Bolshevik leadership.

The two celebrated Red Generals, Budgonny and Voroshilov, accompanied by Stalin, were directed to the Southern Front by the Central Committee. The Wrangel counter revolt, aided by the pygmies on board the "Fearless", was the last forlorn hope of regaining control of the rich Baku oilfield and the coal and steel of the Donetz Basin.

An offensive was launched along the whole length of the Southern Front. A call from Lenin intimated that the Whites and foreign invaders had been resolutely vanquished in all the other theatres of the war in Russia. This was heartening news. But not for Wrangel and his band of bandits — nor for Major Hicks!

The Wrangel Forces made a final stand in the Crimea. Hicks, determined to be in at the kill, entered the Black Sea. Inspired by the promise of loads of loot — and prominence — and well-supplied with booze, he and his motley assembly of crooks and Regulars headed for the Peninsula.

The Red army forced Wrangel southwards and finally bottled the whole White Guard army on the Crimea.

Hicks, approaching the coastline with the destroyer's guns trained on the shore, soon made an expert military appraisal of the position and realised that the Soviet Forces had won the initiative and had completely encircled the Wrangel Army in a pincer from which there was no escape. And Hicks was not about to demonstrate any heroic attempts at relieving a lost cause!

Supported by battalions of armed civilians of the working class from Kiev, Kharkov and the Don Basin, a mighty Red Army was thrown into the final battle which swept the Wrangel Wreckers and the interventionist flotsam into the Black Sea. The Ukraine was cleansed. The Crimea was purified and the whole Imperialist adventure was catapulted into oblivion. The victorious Bolsheviks could now proceed with the relatively unfettered construction of Socialism. The Western and White Guard aspirations of strangling the Soviet system had been ignominiously aborted. The Soviet Government could now pass on to the next item on the Agenda!

At the Belford, wee Hicks stood up in front of his high pew in response to Eglinton-Harris's invitation to speak. He made vague references to his exploits in the Front Line in France during the Great War and enthused about the valuable contribution he could make on the Glasgow streets, based on his wartime experiences. He made a vain effort at a political analysis of the forthcoming Rally.

Eglinton-Harris was becoming embarrassed at the antics of his adjutant. And no wonder. He knew that they were all aware of the fact that he was an alki! And right now, he was as drunk as a puggy!

As he started to gant about his experiences in the "Ruthian" campaign, his top teeth clattered to the polished floor. Dropping to his knees, he reached into his sporran in search of his specs, to find the dentures. Failing miserably on all counts, he attempted a slovenly salute to Edlinton-Harris, while on his arse, and collapsed in a heap!

The bouncer was called in to take him away!

There were giggling guffaws and muted murmurings from the guests, most of whom were not much less drunk than wee Hicks. Eglinton-Harris made the excuses, reminded the guests about the positive features in Hicks' history and spoke of the excessive heat in the conference room! He called for an intermission and lapsed into a conspiratorial conversation with Chief Constable Sillars.

The glasses were topped up and the group broke up into small factions. Before long the fiery effects of the inexhaustible supply of the "cratur" took charge. Gory experiences were exchanged and fantastic flights of fancy were given free rein. Captain Hawkins of the H.L.I. was gassing off about his role in the Russian Intervention period. He had been second-in-command on the abortive expedition to the Crimea with Major Hicks. If ever there was a boastful bum o'hell it was Hawkins. He had seen that he was arousing the interest of the others and went into top gear. His egotism was boundless.

All of the group were aware that the Intervention had been a catastrophe. Hawkins defended his role in the campaign by insisting that if Hicks had accepted his advice, a landing would have been made, "and who knows, our detachment could well have altered the course of history and spearheaded the destruction of the Russian Revolution!" Arnison asked him how he had become attached to Major Hicks in the first place. "I was in his class at the Russian Department in Aldershot. He seemed to have taken a special interest in me. Eventually, he singled me out for special interview. I knew he was on the hunt for a suitable second-in-command for his much vaunted Russian adventure."

The "Brits" in Ireland

Whether on the scaffold high,
Or on the battlefield we die,
What matter, when for Erin we fall.
— *T. D. Sullivan*

SOME of the officers in his class at the Department had gained extensive experience in the suppression of uprisings on the frontiers of the colonies, but Hicks had examined the personal record of Captain Hawkins and he came to the conclusion that he would make an excellent second-in-command. But he wanted to speak to him before making his final selection. "Captain Hawkins, I see from your records that you served a great deal of your military career in Ireland. It also mentions that on at least two occasions you were reprimanded for insubordination, and, in particular, for having taken vital decisions, on your own, without prior consultation with your superior officers. Personally, I am not too concerned about the reasons behind these charges as long as it is clearly understood that if you become my Second, there will be at least one officer who will be superior to you — and that will be me! Now, Ireland is one of the few places that I have not visited on active service. Perhaps you will give me a resumé of just what took place there, when you were recalled and reprimanded. Or was it that you *had* to get out of Ireland?"

Hicks, in fairness, had an educated background, and, on the whole, proved himself to be an obedient and loyal servant of the Crown — an Officer and a Gentleman.

Hawkins was a hooligan! From an early age, he had

developed a deep-seated hatred for anyone who expressed any sympathy with the Irish question. In his warped state of mind all Irishmen were Papes or Fenians. In fact, his allergy even extended to Protestants — if they were Irish.

This unbalanced state of mind was due, in the main, to his upbringing in Springburn where his whole family's narrow-minded fanatical hatred of Catholics had conditioned his mind into an unswerving loyalty to the Flag, King and Country! He joined up.

His expertise as a bully and his obvious qualities as a leader of less confident men assured his relatively early commission. Names like Connolly, Larkin and Parnell were anathema to Hawkins and this malice was suitably exploited by his superiors. The situation in Ireland required men of his calibre. He knew that Hicks would draw him up sharply if he deviated from the truth. He fancied the job of Second, and since Hicks had his record, he had better tread warily.

"Well, Sir, I was in charge of an interrogation unit of the Black and Tans — excuse the expression, sir — at Mountjoy Prison. A Sinn Feiner had been arrested in a derelict shop near Phoenix Park in possession of a number of hand guns. We employed the usual methods of extracting the information required." Hicks interrupted: "Hawkins, I have it on record that you were personally responsible for the near castration of that man while using a bloody blow lamp!"

Hawkins hadn't expected the crude details to be recorded — and presented. He recovered his composure. "With respect, sir, the information we obtained played a major part in the British campaign in Ireland, and furthermore, I think you will see that I was not charged with *that* particular incident. I'm surprised that it is included in my records, sir."

"Oh, go on, for Christ's sake, Hawkins. Between you and me, I don't give a damn about the methods you used."

Hawkins felt that the wee bastard was warming to him. He continued: "As you probably know, the Fenians had carried out a successful raid on the Barracks at Aghavanagh and, with the co-operation of some sympathisers in the Irish Army, looted the armoury and fled into the Wicklow Mountains. We knew, from the man at Mountjoy, that Michael Kane was responsible for the raid. Nine of my men were killed during Kane's attack on the Barracks — apart from the casualties suffered by the Garda and the Irish Regulars.

"You may recall, sir, that the British and Irish Press described the raid as being quite unprecedented and that, to date, it had been the most successful and daring attack yet launched against the Occupying Forces. I lost some good men, sir."

Hicks didn't quite break down and cry, but Hawkins reckoned that he was getting the message — and gaining sympathy.

"In retrospect," he continued, "I probably allowed my emotions to override my status as a responsible Officer of Law and Order. Anyway, I swore to have my revenge!

"Michael Kane and his gang took up strong positions in a village overlooking the Wicklow Gap which forms part of the main road to the South of Dublin. All military movement to the trouble spots in Cork and Queenstown was through this important route. We also knew that Wicklow and Wexford were hotbeds of Republicanism. Kane's men controlled an extremely vulnerable position. The Police and the Irish Army thought it advisable to maintain a low profile in these counties during this incident. They knew damned well that reprisals would be taken sooner or later. So it was left to the Tans, and, in view of what had happened to my men, I accepted the responsibility without question. If I may say so, sir, I think you would have done exactly the same, had you been in my position." Hicks made no comment, and merely nodded assent.

"The information that we had gained at the Mountjoy interrogation proved substantially correct. The I.R.A. in Wicklow were aware that an exceptionally large convoy was due to leave Dublin. It would consist of men and essential materials for distribution along the route to County Cork. The Wicklow and Wexford Groups had been instructed to destroy the convoy by the I.R.A. General Council. In fact, this task was top priority on the hit list of the I.R.A. This was why the Aghavanagh Barracks had been raided.

"I selected thirty experienced men including Sergeant McCluskey. He had spent some valuable time as an undercover man with the I.R.A. since he was Irish, and, in my opinion, an exception to my general rule regarding anything Irish.

McCluskey confirmed the facts supplied by the man at Mountjoy — and more — he presented us with a meticulously detailed plan of the positions to be taken up by the I.R.A. at the Gap. I sent McCluskey back to Wicklow to rejoin their Command and instructed him to keep us posted on any alteration in their plans. I also advised him that, if the opportunity arose, to create a diversion when we mounted our attack. You know, sir, you just couldn't pay enough to a man of that calibre.

"When the convoy was finally assembled, my group took up the leading position in two personnel carriers. We knew, of course, that we were subject to I.R.A. surveillance as we left the city. We expected the observation to ease off as we crossed the city boundary. Intelligence meanwhile, had verified that every available active Republican in Wicklow and Wexford had been drafted into the Wicklow Gap and the surrounding terrain.

"By previous arrangement we increased our lead over the convoy as we left the city limits. When we had attained a three mile lead, we detached ourselves from the convoy at Ballinalea and headed into the hills. It was dusk. A mist was gathering on the slopes as I called for a briefing in a copse of trees a few miles from the village where Michael Kane's men were gathered to prepare for their attack on the convoy.

"As I said, most of my men had been engaged in previous skirmishes so that there was no need to remind them of the no smoking and no talking rule. Four of us had Thomson subs, held by myself, a sergeant and two corporals. Four men had Sten guns. The remainder were armed with the Lee-Enfield .303, with the bayonet in the scabbard. As we prepared to move off, I allocated a number of petrol-filled Guinness bottles, ready primed with candle-wick fuses and cotton rifle cleaner — a particular favourite of mine when launching an attack on an Irish village! I deployed my force in a semi-circle, approaching the village from the rear, thus sealing the place off with no chance of an escape into the hinterland from the edge of the Gap. The encirclement completed, the only outlet available to Kane's men was by the main road.

"The convoy was due at any moment. We knew that the Republicans would be holed up in the cellars, cottages, barns and the village pub which served as a general store. They would

117

be making final preparations for the attack on the convoy. My sergeant and a corporal took up positions at the extremities of the semi-circle. I retained the other N.C.O. A synchronised attack was launched!

"As planned, the incendiaries were tossed on to the cottage roof tops and exposed hay lofts. One or two were directed at the few shop windows. The cottages and hay lofts instantly became infernos. Within minutes the village was engulfed in flames.

"The village and surrounding area became a fiery beacon in the night sky exposing the silhouette of the trees and under-growth on the hillsides. Farm animals bellowed. Trapped horses snickered and neighed in terror. Special attention was directed at the village church — a favourite rendezvous for rebel bands. Screams and shouts rent the night air as the tinder dry cottage roofs were ignited. The Thomsons made short work of hysterical women, clothes ablaze, who fled screaming from the doorways of the cottages, shops and the church.

"The main body of Michael Kane's men appeared from the precincts of a farmyard. Over the crackle of the flames, we heard the rumble of the approaching convoy.

"A large group, presumably led by Kane himself, headed for the slope leading to the main road. With a harsh squeal of brakes, the convoy drew to a standstill thus sealing off our semi-circle. We closed in. The convoy commander saw that we had gained control of the hillside. A few of the rebels gained the slope. Completely exposed by the flames and exploding petrol bombs, there was little need for accuracy of firepower. The staccato spray of bursting bullets from the Stens halted most of them in their tracks. The village street and hillside became a bloodbath of writhing and shrieking men, women and children, their shrill cries piercing the warm night air. Grenades were thrown into the farmyard, outbuildings and the church to dispose of stragglers. The few who managed to reach the road were cut down by a lorry-mounted Vickers as they struggled from the hedgerows and ditches."

Major Hicks was fascinated and nodded admiringly. He readily admitted that Captain Hawkins had a colourful military career and promptly had orders promulgated that would establish him as his second-in-command. He shook hands with Hawkins.

"By the way, Hawkins," he asked, "what happened to your undercover man, Sergeant — what's his name?"

"Oh, that was my only regret, sir. We found Sergeant McCluskey hanging from a beam in a barn. And he had been castrated!"

Final Instructions

HALF of the assembled "Social Committee" at the Belford had fallen sound asleep. The few who had been listening to Hawkins were called to order by the Colonel.

On the basis of all the information, it was decided that the forthcoming Rally warranted the intervention of the military. It was evident, Eglinton-Harris said to his half sleeping drunken audience, that the same influences had been exerted in Glasgow as had been in the Colonies.

Galloway of the Serious Crime Squad was given a free hand. Thus, the military and police leadership of Glasgow, bevvied to the eyeballs with booze, and indulging in an exaggerated orgy of drunken back-slapping compliments on their respective abilities, concluded their conference on how they proposed to deal with the forthcoming threat to the City Administration.

The Raid

> And this I hate — not men, nor flag nor
> race, but only war, with its wild, grinning
> face.   — *Joseph Miller*

THE CIVIL DEFENCE AUTHORITY and the military had commandeered the "Sheepie", a tract of land opposite Firpark Terrace in Dennistoun. At times, the pitch had been roughly marked off and used as a football field by the boys from the local schools. A well-anchored cable behind the East Side goalpost how supported an elephantine barrage balloon whose shining silken form floated like an alien spacecraft above the smoking

119

chimney stacks of Ark Lane and Golfhill. There were two heavily reinforced Nissen-type huts at the opposite end of the former playing field, both of which were streaked with broad sweeping, brown, black and green bands of wartime camouflage paint.

A ten-feet-high "T"-shaped pole carried the terminals, insulators and cables supplying the site with electricity and telephone communication. The heavy gauge corrugated iron doors of the Nissens were secured with a sturdy chain and padlock. An ordinary weatherboarded timber hut ten feet by six accommodated the military staff whose main function was the protection of the two buildings and their contents. Each of the buildings was surrounded by a series of triangular wooden pickets supporting a number of coils of rusted barbed wire.

Red and white War Department notice boards, threatening dire consequences to trespassers, were prominently displayed around the perimeter of the pitch. The barbed wire entanglements, the conspicuous notices and the permanent guard staff betrayed the level of importance attached to the site. This was because the specially strengthened buildings were, in fact, well stocked armouries.

At all times, an armed soldier was stationed in the wooden hut which was heated by a charcoal burning brazier. At regularly defined intervals, the balloon base and the armouries were thoroughly inspected by the soldier on duty.

Olga and Alan had patiently surveyed the installation for three nights from behind a sand dune on the east side of the premises.

Andy had been called in to check the precise method and times of the guard changing procedure. He took up his observation stance at the corner of Golfhill Terrace overlooking the pitch.

The duty sentry, on being relieved, signed a document on a clip board, handed the rifle to his relief and made a telephone call from the telephone hand set mounted on the wall inside the doorway of the guard room.

Andy correctly assumed that the telephone call was confirmation of an uninterrupted change of guard. But he was interested in where the call was being directed. The soldier then mounted the army push bike and, closely followed by Andy's bike travelled along Alexandra Parade, down Castle Street into

Stirling Road and, at Cathedral Street turned into Taylor Street and the military headquarters, thus confirming the route of the telephone link and the location of the supply and personnel depot. The total transfer time between the two points was twenty minutes cycling time.

The post had been filled at two o'clock and had been relieved at eight o'clock in the evening, with subsequent six hourly changes round the clock.

Olga and Alan decided to make the strike on the Thursday night prior to the demonstration on the Saturday morning.

The "Beard" would take up a position adjacent to the massive iron gates leading into the precincts of the Glasgow Cathedral at the Square.

Olga checked the profusion of outbuildings and workshops at the sand quarry and acquired a heavy set of bolt cutters in a fitters tool store which was poorly secured.

They both wore heavy overcoats and Alan had a synthetic silk scarf wound round his neck.

Blackout conditions prevailed, but the whole scene was illuminated in the silvery light of a full moon.

The guard was changed exactly on time.

At half past eight, the soldier emerged from the guard room doorway with the rifle slung over his right shoulder. He circled both of the buildings and returned. At nine o'clock he reappeared and strolled towards the barrage balloon base.

Alan and Olga were crouched behind the lip of the sand dune, within a few yards of the anchorage. The ground was soft and covered with thick brown layers of sand. At the anchorage, the sentry stopped, lowered his rifle, lit a cigarette, opened his greatcoat, loosened his flies — and had a piss!

The silken sheet of the hovering barrage balloon shimmered like a static shining star in the sky and Alan leapt forward. The soldier's rifle was on the ground. Holding the lit cigarette in his left hand, his right hand was busily occupied in manipulating his cock. Alan struck him on the back of the neck with the heavy bolt cutters.

He was still pissing as he struck the soft ground — unconscious. Olga dragged the soldier's greatcoat from his senseless form and dashed towards the barbed wire encirclement at the nearest building.

Alan grabbed the rifle, smashed one of the picket supports

with the butt, while Olga threw the heavy coat over the loosened wire. Alan fell heavily on to the outspread coat and flattened a couple of coils.

Olga ran over Alan's spreadeagled body and headed for the armoury with Alan close behind. The boltcutters soon severed the chain and the door swung open with a piercing shriek of tortured metal.

Entering the armoury, Olga closed the door and cast a torchlight on the rows of shelves and equipment.

The stabbing beam of light reflected the dull sheen of rifle barrels and the fluted black snub of noses of two Bren light machine-guns. The glistening brown stocks and butts of seven .303 Lee-Enfields were picked out by the searching light. Hinged green metal boxes of ammunition were stacked neatly on the shelves with clearly stamped calibre. The remaining equipment consisted of a variety of spare parts for a selection of small arms, some range target materials — and two Mills grenades! Alan was relieved to find that the rifles included the bolt mechanisms. He fully expected the bolts to have been stored separately. Short work was made of the thin chain which had been fed through the trigger guards and padlocked.

This done, Olga went outside, reached upwards with the cutters, and snipped the telephone cables leading to the roof of the guard room. While outside, she directed a single flash of light towards the quarry. Within seconds, three heavily garbed young men dashed across the moonlit pitch. They were each allocated with a rifle and cartons of ammunition, then left the scene. The Bren gun magazines were fully loaded. Alan retracted the bipods, secured the two l.m.g's, one to each end of his scarf, slung the load round his neck and replaced his bulky greatcoat. Olga retained the fully loaded .303 discarded by the sentry, loosened the shoulder strap and secured the weapon lengthwise down her body. She filled her coat pockets with as many cardboard containers of ammunition as she could possibly carry.

Finally, Alan lifted both Mills grenades.

Moving smartly across the deserted site, they linked arms in the manner of a courting couple as they reached Firpark Street. Skirting the gable end of the tenement building, they ambled slowly down the grass track to Wishart Street. Passing the Royal Infirmary laundry, they struggled up and over the railings surrounding the Necropolis. Scrambling through the rows of glistening tombstones and working their way along the protruding buttresses of the Cathedral wall, they finally reached the Square — and the main gates of the cemetery. Olga was completely knackered!

The "Beard" took possession of all of the boxes and rifle, secured a firm foothold on an upper part of the massive gates, leaned and hauled Olga over to the outside of the cemetery, in one quick movement.

The "Beard" hared off towards the Bakunin Hall across the Square. Olga and Alan, resuming their original postures, wandered slowly round the perimeter of Cathedral Square in the shadow of the looking Infirmary and finally crossed Castle Street into the safety of the Hall. The spoils were duly deposited under the floorboards.

Reach for the Skies!

There's villainous news abroad!
— *Shakespeare - Henry IV*

THE two bleary eyed specimens met at the corner of Rottenrow and High Street in the darkness at five o'clock in the morning, and meandered towards the Bakunin Hall.

On opening up, they were pleasantly surprised to find that the big white sheet banner had been laid out and folded neatly for uplifting. Olga had stitched a number of heavy duty brass eyelets to the edges of the enormous banner and had laced them loosely with some short white ropes.

Dougie and Andy were the first of an army of activists and supporters who would be visiting the premises for publicity duties throughout the day and into the late evening hours. A check verified the success of the arms raid by Alan and Olga just a few short hours previously. The arms raid, they agreed, was the most significant stroke yet effected in the campaign. The dormant power inherent in the reclining array of military hardware inspired them to emulate Olga and Alan.

Andy stuffed the folded banner into a *Daily Record* newspaper shoulder bag — a souvenir of his early morning chores as a paper delivery boy. Dougie uplifted a six section milk bottle carrier containing three clinking bottles. Andy jammed a jemmy in his waist belt. They locked up, Castle Street was still quiet.

A railway worker heading for the six-till-two shift at College Goods Station passed the premises as they left. The worker, crouching against the chill morning air, was walking in a cloud of Woodbine smoke.

Keeping pace with the man they headed down into High Street, passing the drab, overpowering grey walls of Duke Street Jail. The first early morning White tramcars were already trundling noisily uphill to Springburn, and south to Polmadie and Netherlee. The rumbling of goods carts and the clumping of horses hooves on the cobbles, could be heard from the gloomy depths of the Goods Yard in High Street. An appetising smell of frying ham and eggs drifted from the darkened doorway of Alstons Tea Room.

The grizzly old newsvendor had already set up his outdoor furniture at the corner of Ingram Street. A fire engine breenjed out of the Fire Station arch and tore along towards the City Centre.

As they approached the Cross the wee cludgie man was opening the underground "Gents". He wore a black, flat topped hat with a shiny skip. The Shite House Attendant's badge of State Authority, Dougie thought. The State loved the Uniform — at any level!

Perhaps it was a measure of his developing political consciousness that he had noticed such an apparent triviality. The Tollbooth Clock faces showed five past six. The city was stirring into life.

Dougie loitered around the south side of the column. The Blue, Kirklee tramcar was just passing the Bridgegate at Saltmarket. It would reach the Trongate in sixty seconds. As it cornered the left turn into the Trongate, it emitted an ear-piercing screech of wheels grinding against a ninety-degree angle of tram rail.

Coincidental with Dougie's hand signal and the high pitched scream of agonised metal, Andy rammed the jemmy into the ancient studded north door of the Tolbooth and wrenched it open. The noise of the splintering timber was unnoticed.

He was joined by Dougie, and they closed the door quickly as they entered the pitch dark interior, wedging it shut with a discarded "Road Up" sign lying just inside.

Working by torchlight, Andy withdrew the banner from the canvas bag, grabbed a short ladder and headed for the top of the Tolbooth steeple. Reaching the breast-high parapets, they were struck by the sheer enormity and height of the structure. They jammed the ladder against the base of the serrated embrasures that circled the perimeter of the tower. At street level there had hardly been a puff of a breeze. Up here, above the height of most of the adjacent rooftops, the wind blowing up the channel of tall buildings that formed Saltmarket, from the Clyde, was like a bloody gale! Dawn was due to break any time.

The wind played merry hell with the once neatly folded banner. In the confusion, they were certain that they were exposed to the whole population!

Following several abject failures to control the capricious folds of the billowing banner they eventually formed a tie at the bottom of the south clock face. Exchanging a few blasphemous pleasantries with the rough grey stonework, their knuckle-tearing efforts finally laced up most of the flapping loose ends.

The two remaining ties forced them to reveal themselves to any interested passing pedestrians or top deck passengers on the passing tramcars. All the ties had been made and the banner fluttered in front of the four faces! They couldn't foresee what effect the clock hands might have on the linen — but they didn't spend any time on contemplation. Leaving the ladder, they made a wild dash to street level, sauntered down towards the Cross Cafe for coffee — and awaited developments.

Effective Publicity

ANDY and Dougie, safely parked at one of the inshot tables in the café, eagerly awaited the outcome of their risky raid on the tower. They could already see early signs of public interest from the doorway of the shop. It was now seven-fifteen and daylight was breaking over the city centre.

Olga, as arranged, had made telephone calls to the desks of the Glasgow newspaper fraternity at six-forty-five from the call box at the Barony Church in Castle Street.

She phoned the *Bulletin*, the *Record*, the *Evening Times*, and *Citizen*. She advised the "heavy" desks at the *Glasgow Herald* and the *Scotsman*.

A special call was made to the Glasgow correspondent of the Communist *Daily Worker*, the only worthwhile, left-orientated newspaper on the news stands.

She informed all of them about the mysterious appearance of the slogan bearing, enormous white banner on one of Glasgow's prominent landmarks!

It is on record, somewhere, that any thrifty Glasgow keelie within viewing distance of the famous big clock faces at Glasgow Cross, wouldn't think of buying a watch! It was even scurrilously suggested that local residents in the proximity of the Tolbooth didn't have a clock!

Confusion reigned at the Tolbooth! Walking workers, heading south to Dixon's Blazes and Dubbs' at Polmadie blinked their bleary eyes in utter disbelief. Passing pedestrians wending their various ways, via the Cross, to Collins and Blackie's the Publishers, and Tennent's brewery, stopped in their stride to study the strident slogans!

The clerical collar and tie brigade seated in the smoke-filled top-decks of the city-bound tramcars from the Gallowgate and London Road cast curious glances at Roxburgh's Revelations. Tram drivers squealed to a halt at one of the busiest traffic intersections in the city.

Newspaper vans and cars snaked their ways to Glasgow Cross from their far flung offices, and disgorged ardent photographers with their paraphernalia and news-hungry reporters at the already congested junction. Car and lorry horns hooted angrily. Tram bells clanged impatiently along the length of Trongate and Argyle Street, mingled with the warbling sirens of police vehicles threading a passage through the throng of trapped traffic in the Saltmarket! Scampering coppers, whistles wailing incessantly, made a concerted rush towards the smashed door of the tower, and quickly removed the offending banner.

Andy and Dougie concluded that the project had been a resounding success, and a perfectly planned propaganda platform!

The Planning

THE GRAPES collection had been more than was expected. Alan was surprised, he had thought that the pub proprietor would have banked such a large amount. But the man had probably decided that it was safer in the premises, especially on a Saturday night.

The money was used for the purchase of extra pamphlets and literature. In the interests of promoting the publicity campaign, and using the windfall of the extra money from The Grapes, the Committee decided to include the names of prominent speakers from the political parties and trade unions, with the inference that a united front in support of Roxburgh and the Federation was accepted. Alan didn't think it likely that the others would object to free advertising on behalf of their stalwarts.

The Labour Party as the main working class organisation developed their campaign to the maximum and promised the attendance of Members of Parliament to their platform. The I.L.P. were rallying their big guns. General Secretaries of leading trades unions would be in attendance, supported by the Red Clyde militants.

They all accepted that the most important attraction would be Jim Roxburgh, and they intended to exploit this to the full — even if he was an Anarchist! He was, internationally and locally a celebrity and deservedly so.

So far, the Anarchists hadn't made a serious impact either in the city or nationally. This, Alan predicted, was about to change! The Federation readily admitted that, in isolation, they were unlikely to exert any real influence, due to the lack of a mass following by the people.

Alan called a meeting in the Bakunin Hall to review the situation. "On our own, it would have been quite impossible to have developed a campaign of this nature and intensity. The whole working class movement in the city has become embroiled in the Rally. What is more, the main, politically-conscious nucleus of the big parties, with the mass support, have pitched in with all of their reserves and will be virtually forced into making a positive contribution to its success. The people will expect this. Furthermore, each will try every trick in the book to out-manoeuvre the others in their attempts to control the leadership. We, of course, must be ready to extract the maximum advantage here. We lack the popular mass support because our aims have been prostituted by the media and the State — but we are undoubtedly correct in our policy, and that's what counts.

"I think the Communist Party will play a major role in drawing the support of the active stewards from the factories and yards. The Young Communist League have drummed up the support of the apprentices committees. Now, I need hardly remind you that the police will be out in force at this demonstration, and this will include the Specials.

"In fact, when the authorities get wind of the breadth of the interest in the march I would not be surprised if they involve the military! Big business is more concerned about the protection of property than they are about people. It is well known that the State will scour the barrel in its efforts to suppress progress. In this connection we should be watchful for the hooligan element of the British Union of Fascists. Their policy will be to denigrate — even destroy — Jim Roxburgh."

The Propaganda Drive

Four hostile newspapers are more to be
feared than a thousand bayonets.
— *Napoleon*

PRIORITY was allocated to the preparation and publication of propaganda materials. Shoals of single sheets were printed on sympathetic presses. Olga took up virtually permanent residence in Bakunin Hall for the distribution of thousands of leaflets, pamphlets and posters. Comrades who had expressed any degree of support for the principles of the Federation, from other organisations, were enticed, inveigled or coerced into participating in the final publicity onslaught.

Every known Anarchist in the city was conscripted to mount a superhuman effort to inundate the heavily populated districts and industrial complexes in the surrounding area.

The propaganda committee had subdivided a large scale map of Glasgow into the most vital catchment sections of the city. Duke Street was deluged from High Street to Parkhead Cross — with emphasis on the Forge. Blochairn and Bishopton were beleaguered by shop stewards and apprentices committees.

Unsuspecting shoppers in the Saltmarket and Stockwell Street were showered with scores of sheets from towering roof-tops. "Bovril" and "Brylcreem" hoardings were mysteriously superimposed with compulsive and colourful, eye-catching posters. Fluttering folios filtered down from the glazed roofs of Central, St Enoch and Queen Street Stations. The City steamies were saturated with sloganised sheets! And so the tempo developed.

Left-wing political parties, seeking the limelight of leadership and initiative launched simultaneously propaganda drives on the shop and shipyard floors and in popular shopping centres. Sympathetic students from Glasgow Technical College and the University demanded a massive presence on the streets on Saturday.

No mention whatsoever had been made, either on the radio networks or in the press, about the raid on the armoury. This omission was very soon rectified. An anonymous telephone caller obliged them with "scant and vague" information regarding a successful assault having been carried through on a military depot in Glasgow on Thursday night! The press immediately investigated this interesting morsel of news, and the editorials "demanded an inquiry". The army and State cover-up had been blown!

Hicks, Hawkins and Sillars suffered slight seizures! A joint communique issued by the military and police authorities denied a cover-up and referred to a break-in at a minor military establishment.

"An investigation is being conducted, but there is no suggestion of a serious breach of National Security."

In fact, every available unit of the Special Investigation Branch had been drafted in to a top-level inquiry into a most serious incident.

The city editors churned out a frantic frenzy of innuendo and demands. A top paper asked, "Is there a Fifth Column in Scotland?" Another suggested "a possible connection of Fascists among the Italian residents in Glasgow."

A second-rate editorial demanded "a more stringent vetting of the conscript army since it is bound to harbour revolutionary and unstable elements who have recently returned from the Republican side in Spain."

The Chief Constable, Sillars, reckoned he knew better, and said so to Superintendent Galloway, the "political expert".

"Bloody papers, how in the name of Christ did they get to know about the armoury?" he said. "I have never seen so many photographs of the Tolbooth and Glasgow Cross in my entire life in the City Force! And somebody is going to get a hard kick in the arse for taking so long to destroy that bloody banner! Alex, this was a particularly well-planned series of operations. I thought you would have had your ear closer to the ground. You knew that bastard was coming here from London, didn't you?"

Galloway nodded assent. He replied:

"The early evening editions are full of it, and you can bet that all of tomorrow's main dailies will have a field day. It is too late now to do anything about that. The damage has been done, and Saturday's copies are already rolling. They know damned well that it has bugger-all to do with the Tallies, a Jerry Spy Ring, or the I.R.A. They know as well as we do that it is down to the Reds and the Anarchists. Anyway as you say, the problem is in my patch. But I tell you that the papers must have got a tip from those responsible. It's obvious that they are seeking political capital and hoping to see signs of a break in our liaison with the Army. It's now five o'clock. There is an awful lot more to this demonstration tomorrow than any of us thought. The arms raid has cast an entirely new and extremely serious complexion on the situation."

Sillars wasn't convinced. He was a worried man. "I have spoken to Hicks and Eglinton-Harris of the military," he said. "You should go now and see Inspector Reilly of the Specials. By the way," he stressed, "as of now, there will be no weekend

130

leave for anyone in the Force. Now, Alex I don't want to enter into precise detail about what your Special Squad should do at the appropriate time tonight. You know well enough who is responsible — and don't, for Christ's sake, ask for warrants if you please — there is no bloody time! I can tell you that we have been well and truly grabbed by the short hairs this time!"

Revolt

Let the ruling classes tremble at a Communist revolution. The proletarians have nothing to lose but their chains. They have a world to win! Working men of all countries unite!
— *Marx and Engels*

SATURDAY dawned with the city centre air clear, crisp and dry. Barrage balloons speckled the sky like big, fat silver sausages in the wintry morning sunshine. Bus loads of coal miners and their families were already converging on Glasgow from Blantyre, Cambuslang, and from as far as Shotts in the Lanarkshire coalfield.

The Scottish miner, the cream of the British working class was, as usual, in the forefront of any progressive development or demonstration affecting the trade union movement. Historically, and second to none in the records of militancy, the Scottish collier would again, today, be first to unfurl the red banner of Labour.

Groups of young students marched towards the City Centre, chanting slogans and carrying the flags of the University Union and political party placards.

Labour Party branches from the city and sururban constituencies progressed along Parliamentary Road, Crown Street and Gallowgate led by prominent figures from London, Edinburgh, and Glasgow.

Trade unionists from the steel industry in Motherwell and from the shipyard on the Clyde, preceded by works pipe bands marched proudly with forests of flying flags.

The Communist Party and the Young Communist League had mustered the most active shop stewards and apprentices.

Committees strode under their flowing crimson banners depicting vivid likenesses of Harry Pollitt, Stalin and Willie Gallacher. Alan, Dougie and Jim Roxburgh, accompanied by a few other Glasgow Anarchists, appeared in Blythswood Square at half past nine.

Party and union branch secretaries and chairmen scampered around feverishly with loud hailers trying to create some semblance of order and discipline among the rapidly multiplying crowds of workers and students.

The major attraction, of course, was Jim Roxburgh, and Glasgow was determined that the traditional label of the "Red Clyde" would not be tarnished by any lack of militancy.

Roxburgh was borne shoulder high and placed in front of the massive snaking column of cheering demonstraters as it weaved ponderously into Blythswood Square.

By ten o'clock, the Square was bursting at the seams and parallel marches were forming up in West Nile Street, Buchanan Street and North Frederick Street from the overflow of people forced to disembark from packed buses and tramcars that had travelled in to the centre from the north and east. As the cascade of workers descended southwards, it was confronted by a solidly packed George Square.

A path was cleared for the main Jim Roxburgh procession, and on its arrival, the Anarchist Federation set up the speakers' podium on the broad pavement facing the City Chambers and adjacent to the Cenotaph.

Roxburgh, obviously impressed by one of the most powerful demonstrations that he had ever witnessed, proved to be in fine fettle and delivered an eloquent and vigorous statement calling for an immediate end to all unjust wars — including the current imperialist war. He appealed for a temporary united front of the whole Labour and trade union movement to bring this to fruition.

Analysing the structure of the State and its organs of repression, he directed the vast crowd's attention to the menacing khaki-clad figures on the surrounding rooftops and to the excessive Regular and Special Police presence ranged around the perimeter of the Square.

Relating his favourite theme, he maintained that the military force at this public demonstration proved beyond a doubt that the *wresting* of power was insufficient and demanded its absolute destruction!

It was now eleven o'clock.

A group of young Communist students started a high-pitched chant of "Down with the Imperialist War" and Smash the State", which was gradually and inexorably taken up by the thousands of demonstrators who had by this time been swelled with waves of slogan-shouting marchers in Cochrane Street and Miller Street who had travelled from the south side. The chant was abbreviated as it was elevated into a tremendous roar of "Down with the War and the State!", "Down with the War and the State!"

A solid blue barrier of police fronted the main entrance to the City Chambers, while two ranks of Specials completely sealed off the entrance to Queen Street Station. Behind the Specials, in the station forecourt, was a posse of two dozen, mounted policemen.

A Labour Party speaker with a loud hailer announced that a skirmish had broken out between a group of workers and police at the front of the High Court, opposite the Green.

It was confirmed that a heavy force had been dispatched from the Central Office to prevent an extra large procession of iron and steel workers from the plants in the south from reaching the Square.

There was a report of a pitched battle at the North British Locomotive works in Springburn, where the shift workers had downed tools and were conducting factory gate meetings prior to a march on George Square.

It was half past eleven.

Communications Failure

THE "BEARD" and another, younger Anarchist, overpowered, gagged and roped up the two uniformed security guards at Dalmarnock Power Station.

The shift control engineers were instructed, at gunpoint, to isolate the whole network of electricity sub-stations supplying the south side of the Clyde and adjoining districts.

They were assisted in this operation by a number of sympathetic members of the Electrical Trades Union working in the station. At precisely the same time, other groups of armed activists carried out similar raids at Pinkston and Braehead Power Stations, and at the City's Transport Supply Depots. The City tramway system ground to a screeching halt. The underground circuit trains stopped dead in their tracks. Shift working machinery in Weir's of Cathcart, Parkhead Force and the engineering shops throughout the industrial complex on the River Clyde shuddered to a standstill!

The main line railway signalling system was totally incapacitated. The primary and secondary telecommunications stations were visited and promptly disconnected. Newspaper printing presses were paralysed. Liaison between the city police stations and all military establishments was shattered. Production ceased abruptly at all of the Royal Ordnance Factories. Local Government administration became impotent! The Second City ceased to function and was virtually isolated from the rest of the country!!

All of the speakers' voices were being drowned in the swelling roar of defiance and objection to the increasing military strength which was rapidly becoming more obvious — and aggressive! There were occasional flashes of light being reflected from the polished steel bayonet blades peering over the rooftop edges, alongside the black snub noses of the rifles.

Andy mounted the pedestal of one of the numerous monuments in the Square, waving wildly in an attempt to concentrate the people's attention on the troops. The crowd glanced upwards, shielding their eyes with cupped hands against the bright wintry sunshine. This was when they realised that the soldiers had been drawn from the ranks of the Highland Light Infantry. That, in all probability they would be conscripts! And there was no doubt that the threatening forces had been posted here from Maryhill Barracks. Certainly they would be Scotsmen — and native Glaswegians! Thousands of upturned eyes and raging voices demanded their immediate withdrawal from the scene. A thunderous concerted roar of disapproval called for the troops to lay down their arms.

Steel helmeted figures, aware that they had been placed in a contradictory and embarrassing predicament, backed away, hesitantly, from the parapets. Was it possible that they, Glasgow workers in uniform, would fire on their fellow workers? Some of the soldiers could be seen struggling and fighting with each other on the rooftops.

A perfectly ridiculous figure — obviously an officer — brandishing a pistol and gesticulating frantically like a prancing puppet, made a frenzied but fruitless effort to restore discipline in his recalcitrant ranks.

The deafening din of the crowd drowned out the voices of the wavering troops, their feinting figures resembling a staged puppet theatre show on the sunlit skyline.

But a pistol shot was fired and a soldier fell backwards, his legs trapped in a crevice on the edge of the roof. Hanging like a limp rag doll, his helmet and rifle bounced crazily on the window ledges, all the way down the face of the building.

The vast crowd, aghast, fell silent.

A bayonet flashed, and the officer's head was almost severed from his body!

Two H.L.I. soldiers lifted the mangled form by the arms and feet and in a swinging count of three, tossed the corpse earthwards into the seething mass of demonstrators.

As though in response to a pre-arranged signal a squadron of the Kings Own Yorkshire Light Infantry, shouldering arms, was seen heading westwards along George Street towards the Square. Just then, a phalanx of truncheon wielding coppers appeared from beneath the arches in lower John Street and, marching in parallel with the predominantly English soldiers, struck out for the nucleus of the mass of demonstrators — Jim Roxburgh's podium!

Memories of the police, the military — including the armoured cars — and the fluttering Red Flag of 1919 flooded back to the minds of some of the veteran trade unionists. And they vividly recalled the proclamation of the Riot Act from the steps of these City Chambers.

The Spark!

Two small boys found space enough to enjoy a closely confined game of hick-the-can with a rounded chip of concrete on the pavement area at the west end of the Square. They were booting the chip from one to the other behind the line of outward facing police when the concrete block was inadvertently skited through the big plate glass window in the bank building.

There was an ear shattering crash of heavy gauge "Bank" embellished glass.

All hell broke loose!

The posse of police horses in the station forecourt whinnied with fright, reared upwards on their hind legs and unceremoniously couped their posturing riders, arse over tit, on to the cobbled court, slithering in fresh horse shit and screaming crude oaths and vile curses at all and sundry! The panic-stricken horses careered wildly into the station and disappeared along the platforms, forcing terrified porters and ticket collectors to make flying leaps on to the railway tracks. A few horses, quite uncontrollable, charged through the double line of foot police, scattering the coppers like ninepins into the tightly packed crowd.

The people immediately suspected that an organised mounted police charge was under way — and this wasn't entirely unexpected. At this point the marching coppers in George Street had reached the outer edge of the densely packed rally, waded in with raised batons and started to cut a ruthless swathe towards Roxburgh and his comrades.

Olga was lying spreadeagled on the dusty floor of the loft in a derelict warehouse building a hundred yards up North Frederick Street, her eye straining through the sights of her Bren gun.

The l.m.g. was mounted on an upturned empty tea chest with the end of the barrel poking through a broken window-pane. When she saw the violence being wreaked on the defenceless crowd, and the imminent danger to Jim Roxburgh and his supporters by the police and the closely following infantry, she loosed off a sharp burst of bullets from the Bren into the solid ranks of the assailants who were now clobbering the crowd with bloodstained batons and rifle butts.

The totally unexpected spurt of fire halted the attackers in their tracks, while half a dozen mutilated uniforms lay prone in their midst.

They were soon surrounded and hemmed in by the seething crowd. Unable to retreat the troops and police reacted even more violently and lashed out on the heads and shoulders of the people. Roxburgh incited mass resistance to the unprovoked attack!

Olga abandoned the Bren and made her escape by running along the length of the building, kicked open an emergency door, and clattering down an external stairway, vanished into the milling mass halfway up North Frederick Street.

A platoon of Yorkshires was directed towards the building and were forced to use the same tactics as the main group, since the people, now thoroughly provoked at the atrocities being committed in the Square, set up a solid resistance to their progress.

As the platoon struggled to reach the old warehouse Dougie, at the other end of the Square, lobbed a hand grenade down into the basement area of the City Chambers in Cochrane Street. The explosion, in the confined space of the well of the basement, blew a hole through the wall and hurled bricks, metal and clouds of dust into the upper street level.

Power to the People!

A reform is a correction of abuses;
a revolution is a transfer of power.
— *Bulwer-Lytton*

AS THE CRASH of the explosion reverberated around the Square, a deathly foreboding stillness descended on the densely packed mass of people. Everyone looked upwards towards the towering rooftops, half expecting a fusillade of fire. Suspicious eyes surveyed the perimeter of George Square, not quite knowing what lay in store for them. And this was when they became fully aware of their invincible latent strength! The organs of repression had been smashed and the remnants outmanoeuvred. The United Front that Roxburgh had demanded, had been firmly established.

The whole vast assembly of workers, students and demonstrators became a surging, angry mass intent on revenge. There was a rustle of revolution in the electrified air! An unyielding circle of activists surrounded the Roxburgh platform!

Roxburgh seemed to have found a new inspiration and called, stridently, for the complete exploitation of the changed situation. The people were in control! They were infuriated, and trampled the khaki and blue uniforms into the ground like so many blood sucking gnats, by their sheer force of numbers. Shots criss-crossed the Square. The people became more enraged! Hundreds of workers fell on the assailants, overwhelmed, and destroyed them.

Rifles were passed from hand to hand and transferred to the men encircling the platforms most of whom, including Roxburgh, had experienced the war in Spain and were fully qualified in their use.

The political aspirations of the numerous activists in George Square differed radically.

The aims of the Anarchists were clearly defined and unswerving. The final solution — the destruction of State Control — could not, they maintained, be compromised.

The Communists, intent on revolution, bloody or otherwise, and conscious of their role as the vanguard of the workers uprising, recognised that control of the administration in isolated Glasgow was within their grasp.

Assault on the Citadel!

THE ANARCHIST FEDERATION and the Communist Party (historically the most politically experienced of the various groups participating in the demonstration) had, nevertheless, maintained a strong cohesion of ultimate interests throughout the campaign, especially among the younger elements of both groups.

Radical differences in dogma existed within the respective leaderships. But a United Front had been created — albeit temporarily — based on the combined operations of youth of both organisations. Their united action had initiated the mightiest demonstration of workers ever seen in Scotland. United, they had procured the finances — and the arms. Working together, they had immobilised and isolated the City of Glasgow. Jointly, they recognised the fundamental difference in the current situation from that which existed in the near-revolutionary crisis in 1919; the presence of a competent and united leadership — in the field! At this historic moment in the destiny of this great City, each complemented the other.

Armed to the teeth, the combined forces stormed the final bastion of helmeted, baton battering police ranks defending the City Chambers — and dissolved them!

The ornate doors of vested authority were smashed to smithereens, and the Forces of Revolution descended on the seat of power.

Two flags snapped and cracked in the wind of change which blew over the roof of Glasgow City Chambers on parallel poles.

The Jet Black Flag of Anarchism and the triumphant Rectangle of Red, bearing the Hammer and Sickle of Socialism!